BUILD A BRAND NEW YOU!

Build a BRAND New YOU!
A Step-by-Step Guide to Launching a Successful Business

ISBN: 979-8-9909888-0-4 (Hardcover)
ISBN: 979-8-9909888-1-1 (Paperback)
ISBN: 979-8-9909888-2-8 (eBook)

*This book is dedicated to my loving husband.
Thank you for all your support, long hours,
late-night sacrifices and commitment. Your strength,
encouragement, and intelligence have been instrumental in
making this project a success. I am beyond blessed to have
you by my side through it all and on our continued
journey in life and in business together.*

WARNING!

What's going to set you apart from your competition is **YOU**. You are unique! There is no other person like you in the world so the competition is obsolete. By you picking up this book you've already set yourself apart from the 80% of people that will not take the extra steps to crush it in their industry. We currently live in a society where people who are curious will go out of their way to look things up and google it. As a matter of fact, so many people are sharing business strategies, products or services like you online and you can't help but wonder, "where do I fit in this world?' "How do I compete?"

Well, I am here to tell you that there is no secret. So, if you think you have this amazing offer… so does everyone else. You might be like many business owners and entrepreneurs who are distracted by the noise and missing critical key steps to building a solid and sustainable business that is different, organic and authentic from everything else out in the market. The problem we see most is skipping those in between steps to lay the groundwork and connect the dots that are necessary to keep your business thriving in a very competitive world. You've come to the right place. You are going to have a hard time putting this book down!

BUILD A BRAND NEW YOU!

STEP-BY-STEP GUIDE TO LAUNCHING A SUCCESSFUL BUSINESS

FORWARD

Hey there, ROCKSTAR!

It's great to meet you! Let me formally introduce myself. I'm a devoted wife, a mother of four daughters and six grandchildren, and a servant of God. In my twenties, I was a struggling stay-at-home mom who couldn't go to work because daycare would cost me more than what I could make. The other option would have been to work a midnight job, but I would never get to see my husband or get any rest, and it would have caused more stress than I already had. I was blaming myself for not contributing. So, I decided to go back to school to become a nurse, thinking that would be the solution to our problem, as I was brought up in the traditional world of going to college to become somebody - work 40 hours a week for 40 years to retire on 40% of my income. That would certainly set us up... yeah, right!!

AS A YOUNG STAY-AT-HOME MOM, HOW WAS I GOING TO PULL THIS OFF WITH NO EXPERIENCE OR FORMAL EDUCATION, WHILE LIVING IN A STRUGGLING ECONOMY, TO FIND SUCCESS IN NETWORK MARKETING?

I was paying student loans and was more in debt than when I started. I didn't even pursue work in what I went to school for because I found out that I was serving sick care instead of healthcare. It really made me second guess what I was called to do.

FINDING MY CALLING...

I knew I had a passion to help people, but I had to figure something out quickly since my husband was in and out of the hospital with a congenital heart condition, facing the loss of his job due to that and unfortunately a struggling economy. I decided to pursue other ways to make extra income, and it led me to health and wellness in network marketing. Little did I know that my past education in medicine, alongside my direct/network marketing experience, would help propel me in my business.

Everything just seemed to align, but it really did sound too good to be true. At first, I was very skeptical, still not knowing what I had gotten myself into, and not believing that the income stories I'd heard could happen to me. But it couldn't be any worse than what I was already going through, and I knew I had no other options; this had to work!

SOMETHING CLICKED...

I later learned that the network marketing business model in health and wellness took ordinary people and helped them to achieve extraordinary results from their health to their finances. I was hooked, and my belief was unshakeable.

To my surprise, I surpassed a nurse's salary by age 43. I was earning an income that rivaled my husband's six-figure salary in the I.T. industry. As a matter of fact, I recall a day where I made $10,000 in four hours.

I've won company-sponsored contests, I've paid off two BMWs, and I'm living in my dream home with all the bells and whistles that I never could afford before.

Today, as an established entrepreneur with over 25 years of experience, I've been able to harness that experience and implement strong systems to build a large successful team, and to my surprise, I've been able to do this full-time and have never looked back at a J.O.B. (Just Over Broke). I was even able to master and build up my expertise as a web designer in my own IT company (WebBot Designs) for over 22 years. Combining my knowledge in technology with my business and marketing experience has propelled me as a brand strategist and brand marketing professional and has allowed me to understand the intricacies of effective online marketing to crush it in the social media scene. I've led several businesses, large companies and organizations, and have been instrumental in the growth and success of many others.

NOW, I AM IN CONTROL OF MY OWN DESTINY, AND I HAVE COMPLETE TIME FREEDOM! I CAN SHOW YOU HOW TO DO THE SAME.

I've appeared in several speaking engagements where I've been able to educate, motivate, and inspire people on my commonsense approach to business and have the ability to reveal the untapped hidden potential of my clients and revive businesses and companies that were looking to give up.

See, it wasn't until a few months into 2024 did I have an awaking, that "a-ha" moment. I was living with the idea of network marketing being a must in order to survive as a back-up plan, a plan B to get people out of their plan A – J.O.B. (Just Over Broke), not realizing that a plan B that I was building was supposed to be my plan A. The old idea is that a plan B is what you work on in case plan A falls apart. The fact is that what you focus on becomes your plan A. If you focus on plan B, plan A will never work out. If you apply it to how most people build network marketing, the plan A becomes the business that people are building to get out of their J.O.B. (their safety net or plan B).

All the while, mind you, I was building my integrity, character, leadership and marketing skills and was having success in my IT company as a result of it, which allowed for both my husband's and my talent and purpose to come through.

Each and every one of us don't realize there is a talent within us. We tend to ignore it or not act on it, feeling that we are not good enough. You know that feeling, the fear of success. What if we do get successful? How could we handle the overload? That was me.

Then I realized that we were allowing careers and circumstances to dictate our future when all along we had our future right in our hands and that we truly were in control. We didn't have to work for someone else. We could be the company that worked for ourselves. We could determine our income versus depending on someone else determining it for us. Now don't get me wrong, I will stand behind any good network marketing company for someone who is building their plan A or an ultimate side gig to bring in the extra income.

But if you understand network marketing, you can really go about it yourself to have your own business if you have it in you to go that route. I was constantly beside myself and beating myself up on the idea as to what was wrong with me - why I was feeling like I was spinning my wheels. If my product is so awesome, and I had the experience to be successful, why was I stagnant in my network marketing business? If you can relate, have you ever wondered that yourself?

That "a-ha" moment was when I realized that I had such a passion for business – I lived, ate and dreamed it - but the "a-ha" was the business I was putting all my passion into was not mine! I was growing someone else's dream. I thought, "so what if I can do it on my own and help my husband get out from working for a job that is slowly pushing him out due to age and being at the top pay tier?" Companies can pay less for recent college students or grab someone offshore for his position. It's a crazy and unsettling world we live in. So, we decided to get to work and just like that we had an overnight breakthrough. Because - in the end - no one was coming to save us and no one is coming to save you but you. It's time to start living for yourself!

My purpose as a professional brand strategist, digital marketer, blogger, web designer, global trainer, and recruiter is to position you in the marketplace to maximize marketing efforts, generate leads, and increase income without sacrificing your time and to show you how to avoid the mistakes and major pitfalls most people make in business.

"Build a BRAND New You!" fills in the gap between having a business idea to building a solid business identity that turns people who would otherwise pass by into a tribe waiting to buy from you. I get it, you just don't have the time to figure it all out on your own, only to be left behind.

My goal is to create YOU an authentic brand identity that sets you apart from your competition, creating financial security that YOU literally own, where you can pass the legacy on to your loved ones to continue the generational wealth. Today, my husband and I have reached top levels in network marketing and have coupled that with our IT company to earn a multi-six figure income in our businesses. We enjoy the freedom of traveling the world together, meeting awesome people, dining out, shopping, and not having to guard every nickel. It doesn't get any better than that, and I would love to do the same for you. I have always believed in giving 100% with zero expectations because one: no one can ever let you down when doing that, and two: the more you give, the more blessings you receive.

I'm finally living the life that most people only dream about. My husband and I believe that God puts you where He wants you.

Let's face it, we are living in a fast-paced environment and it's easy to be distracted in this crazy, noisy, and ever-evolving busy world, and get discouraged to even want to start. I totally understand that time is money. As a busy professional, you may not have the extra time to keep trying to figure it out. Your grabbing my book was definitely no accident. You are here for a reason. If I can add simplicity and value to your life then this book is a sure fit. I'm excited and looking forward to serving you, helping you take the guesswork out and meeting you at your needs. You are not just jumping on the latest marketing trend here. I want to eliminate the problem we see most and that is overlooking the fundamentals of building a brand, a solid business foundation and knowing who you are so that you can finally have long term success instead of continually chasing the next best thing.

It's time to BOSS UP! You have a business to run!

Yours to count on!

CONTENTS

CONTENTS

INTRODUCTION

ARE YOU IN BUSINESS?

3... 2... 1... The cutting of the ribbon has commenced. It's day one and you just opened the doors to your new establishment or online business. But. . .

"Why does it feel like crickets?"

"Did I open too soon?"

"Why isn't everyone just as excited as I am?"

"Surely, everyone can see that what I offer is, in fact, what everyone needs, but why do I feel like everyone is avoiding me?"

"Has my reach all of a sudden become small?

"Is my offer, product, service, or opportunity becoming just like any other?"

"Am I not good enough to compete with the best in my industry?"

"How am I going to create attraction and keep up with the current trends on how to market on social media to keep me afloat?"

Listen, I totally get it!!
Let me ask you an important question…

ARE YOU TRULY OPEN FOR BUSINESS?

You see, many entrepreneurs, business owners and busy professionals miss a few important key elements and critical steps to creating an authentic brand identity necessary to set themselves apart from the competition. Although we want to take our business into what is current and trending today, the problem I see most is skipping those in between steps where we want to jump right into what is new without laying the groundwork that will keep your business moving solidly. We tend to put the cart before the horse and don't anchor ourselves with a solid plan, losing sight of purpose, which leads to fear of failure. Fear, in turn, can close you up and block off all the opportunities to grow and all the avenues leading to your dream becoming reality.

HAVING THE PATIENCE FOR SOMETHING YOU REALLY DESIRE, WILL FEEL THAT MUCH BETTER WHEN YOU FINALLY ATTAIN IT.

I can promise that the people who have paved the way had to set their foundation in place before anything else. As a matter of fact, some of us have big dreams – the "why", the thing that gets you out of bed. Surely, if

3

something is that important, you would rate that a 10, right? By rating your dreams a 10, it's because you know that you know. You are sure about your dreams and that is the one thing that will get you out of bed and will move you.

But if I asked you to rate your foundation and the process you have in place to get it done, the thing that you put in place to achieve your dreams, what would you rate that? Would you rate that a 10 as well? Better yet, what would you rate your potential?

This is the reason why most people don't get their business off the ground or don't achieve their dreams. They just don't have the foundation to support it. Likewise, if your dreams are above your potential then you have to raise your potential to surpass the level of your dreams. We dream big and lose sight of potential because we don't believe we are worthy of it.

When you don't seize the moment and embrace your potential or the changes that come with discovering your calling and talents, do you know what happens? You start losing sight of who you really are and risk losing opportunities. This can lead to a sense of self-abandonment in your authentic self. Before you know it, you're stuck in a mold that doesn't even fit you or who you want to become, creating an alternative life path that deviates from your true potential. We all crave a sense of belonging and validation, but it's important to stay true to ourselves and not get lost in the pursuit of external approval.

Understanding these critical steps can make a huge difference in the way you function daily by building a strong foundation to support your dream and transform your potential to turn your dreams from "Someday" into "I WILL!"

It's easy to get complacent in the process. It's like playing a video game. It can be very frustrating to have to go through the game levels before getting to the finish line, but when you do, you have an idea of what to expect if you had to play the game again. Some people have a hard time getting past the game levels because of an instant gratification mentality, the "I want it now" syndrome. But setting your foundation and putting the proper systems in place are the things that are going to set you apart. Patience is a virtue, a commodity that we should all learn to grab a hold of. I am so glad you made the decision to grab my book, your very first step in eliminating fear, raising the bar, and going to the next level, making that simple tweak that can put you above everyone else. My goal is when you implement what you will learn in this book, your foundation will grow to meet your dream and your potential exceeds so that you can continue and move on to even bigger dreams.

My book is a step-by-step guide designed to launch your business right in today's market, show you how to avoid the mistakes and major pitfalls most people make in business. Most importantly teach you how to create raving fans who are ready to chase you down for your offer and can't wait to be a part of your tribe.

The biggest mistake we make is thinking we have competition out there that can take us down. Yes, there are other business owners who may have paved the way, but their ideas are not the same as yours.

Let's take a look at the music industry. Why do people continue to make music? There's already so much out there. Why keep adding new artists to the lineup? People already have their favorites. It's an ever-growing industry, and it's never going to stop because people, in general, are designed to be curious. And with so many genres to choose from, we have endless options. There's always room for more. Well, the same can apply to your business. If you stay in your lane and put the same effort that you spend worrying about what others are doing, or what they are saying about you into concentrating on learning and building your business and creating your brand identity that stands out. When you focus on your business and become an expert in your field, you will find the crowd meant for you that will become your tribe, designed for your offer. It is so important to be intentional when making the move to take your business to the next level. When you can get to a point in your business where you specialize in it and start becoming the go-to authority that can lead others to success as well, this is where you will start to see the enhancements with credibility and growth where you can start expecting an increase with your industry recognition and a following like no other. So, whether you have a business or a side gig in network marketing, you will start to find your own talents aside from those mentioned that can turn into a business of your own that will cultivate into a paid opportunity.

CHAPTERONE

KNOW YOUR INDUSTRY AND YOUR PLACE IN IT

All too often, I hear people get so excited about owning their own business, like a brick-and-mortar business, or have a great business idea or concept, but they're just not quite sure where or how to start. Maybe they've started but wonder if they're on the right track. Or they're simply looking to grow and expand locally by learning online attraction marketing through social media with engagement, activity, and customer relations. Can you relate? I totally understand how launching your business can be overwhelming and create fear. Sometimes, you start second guessing whether you should do it and never really get your business off the ground and launched, resulting in missed opportunities. Rest assured that you have already made the biggest step that you will ever go through in your business, which is taking the risk and investing in your success.

IF YOU DON'T BELIEVE THAT YOUR OFFER IS IN HUGE DEMAND OR BELIEVE THAT YOU ARE AN AUTHORITY IN THE FIELD OF YOUR BUSINESS, HOW SUCCESSFUL DO YOU THINK YOU WILL BE TRYING TO CONVINCE PEOPLE TO BUY FROM YOU?

Knowledge is key, so we should always be investing in

ourselves and continuing to sharpen our axe. If you want to be at the top of your industry, you have to keep up with the trends. Now, I didn't say you have to be like everyone else, but never hesitate to emulate those before you to help yourself get ahead. Remember that you are unique and different. Be sure to take advantage of that. Legacy leaders are paving the way and sharing secrets for you to be successful, just like leaders have done before them.

They all have laid strong foundations to get to that point to take the guesswork out for you. Now, don't get me wrong, I have seen successful people who shortcut their way and get lucky, just by offering their products or services without creating their foundation or implementing the critical steps to be successful. There are even a few who don't even have it together. They have no foundation as to who they are or what they stand for, like a company name or logo, etc. It's like when we were younger, and we babysat, telling our neighbors about our babysitting gig in the hope that they'll trust us to do a good job. This, right here, is why you will only see 10% make it to the top. They are willing to do whatever it takes to be successful by doing it right and never taking shortcuts. I see the shortcut mentality more often in the network marketing industry. It's easier when you are working with a company because you can always put the blame on them if you don't have results rather than putting the blame on your own efforts to go to work. I also notice that customers will feed off of their excitement and buy into their sales tactics, if you will. However, no one wants to be sold to, and that initial success starts to fade out when the consumer realizes that the buying hype has faded when they got home. They start wondering what they've done and talk themselves out of what they bought. They never really become true consumers. There is something to be said when YOU own your own business, and the accountability is solely on YOU. Although it's easy enough to start with hype, keeping business on the books will become an issue and the company retention suffers.

The truth is, if you are going to get your customers feeding off your excitement, don't sell the company; sell them on YOU. No one is going to buy anything you have until they can develop a relationship and can trust you. You see, it doesn't always start with marketing your offer, really. It begins with engaging like-minded individuals that you have something in common with and creating long-lasting relationships and your brand identity that people can relate to genuinely, which is the key factor in creating longevity, proof, credibility, and trust. Your goal should be that when you launch this incredible company, it will be here for years to come and will grow exponentially where you can leave that legacy with your family and loved ones to carry on the name, right?

Sometimes, I hear of brick-and-mortar companies that have been around for decades and have not grown to their full potential, or that people join a network marketing company and they're selling the company name and not their own when, in fact, they are the business owner. So, whether you decide to be an entrepreneur working with a company, or decide to branch out on your own, you need to be clear that you aren't selling the company. Remember, products can sell themselves off the shelf. Have you noticed that many department stores will carry the same item? Why should I buy at a particular store for that item? Why do we choose our favorite grocery store to shop?

The reason…**TRUST** and **GREAT EXPERIENCE**. Keep in mind, they didn't sell the product. They sold themselves as being the household name that everyone grows to love. If I were to ask you to look into a mirror and then ask, "would you buy from you?" would you?

If you have not clearly identified your target audience early on, it could make things very difficult to take the steps to develop your brand identity. Unfortunately, most people skip this important step because it can be very difficult to read people and to cater to different personalities in order to convey your message.

KNOWING YOUR INDUSTRY AND YOUR PLACE IN IT IS SO VITALLY IMPORTANT TO THE SUCCESS OF YOUR BUSINESS. IT'S ALSO ABOUT BEING AWARE OF YOUR CLIENT OR TARGET AUDIENCE THAT INCLUDES YOUR COMPETITORS!

If you consider starting your brand creation by listening to what your audiences are looking for and what connects them to the process, as well as your competitors' strengths and ideas, you can use that to cultivate a unique and authentic niche while capitalizing on their weaknesses. This will make it that much easier to move forward in designing a brand that resonates with those who can relate to and engage in your offer.

CHAPTERTWO

CREATE YOUR BRAND, LOGO, AND IDENTITY

Knowing your brand starts with a few very important questions.

"Simply put… who are you?"

"What do you stand for?"

"What do you want people to remember you as?"

"What do you want to be known for?"

We know that people, in general, all have a uniqueness about them, from personality, to style, and values. But what lasting impression do you want to leave that person, client, or customer that you can be proud of? Your brand identity is the DNA make up of your brand. If you ask yourself these questions, what can you say about your business that will leave your customers with a memorable and unforgettable experience, that if they came across your brand identity without seeing you physically there, would they recognize and know it was you?

What's so scary about businesses today is that so many entrepreneurs miss this critical key element in business or dismiss it thinking it's not needed, whether it's a side gig or a primary source of income. It is very important to have a brand identity. It's not enough to say that you have an online business presence, It has to be rooted in an identity that people can connect with. Now, I am not saying that your brand identity is based on what you see. It's a much deeper emotional connection than that. It has a lot to do with relatability and matching characteristic traits to your customers.

When you combine all this and interact with a customer's emotions and experience in a way that you can impact their lives, then you start cultivating a brand that leaves them wanting more. Is any of this making sense? When you look in the mirror... would you want to buy from yourself?

LET'S DO IT RIGHT AND OFFICIALLY LAUNCH YOUR BUSINESS LIKE A ROCKSTAR

Whether you are an existing company, a new company just starting out, would like to start a brick-and-mortar business, or are simply looking to work a side gig, like network marketing, you have to have a strong, solid foundation as to why you are doing it in the first place, how you will effectively do it and what your business day to day operations is going to look like. Because being a business owner comes with daily disciplines and responsibilities already, it can be very difficult to run without having a solid system and plan in place. Especially when most people today work from their mobile devices or remotely, it requires major discipline to work from home. So, to know who you are, what you stand for, and how your day-to-day operations will be implemented are vital and critical to running a successful business. Now, we have identified what your brand identity should look like. It's a culmination of how you want people to see your brand summed up by creating a name for your company.

Let's start with **CREATING A NAME FOR YOUR COMPANY.**

Your name is your first impression to your customers and can make a huge difference in how you brand yourself. Be creative, but don't complicate it. You want a name that carries weight and tells people exactly who you are and the sum of your identity. Don't make them do mental gymnastics to figure out what you're in business for. It is so important to get it right, and to create a strong identity. How are people going to find you easily online? Think about the words you would look for when finding a company that does what you do. Whether you are a store front traditional business or an online only presence, the reality is we need to start from a traditional business mindset and move it onto an online presence.

By envisioning it, it's going to help in creating the idea of your company name - nothing too long, but something catchy and memorable.

You also want something in the name that is an easy keyword search that makes it much more visible to your target audience when looking for you online. Choose a name that distinguishes your business. A name that will shake up the competitors in your industry and grab the attention of your audience. The world as we know it today is interconnected digitally, and we need to lead with that in mind.

The internet is good at watching people and their interests. Have you ever noticed that every time you search for something, it's suddenly all over your social media platforms?

Your search lets A.I. and Google bots know what you are into. Then, it connects what you view to your search. If you love makeup, it will send you a barrage of makeup ads and information. The idea is to be among those in your niche and be listed as well. But be aware of trendy names.

I have seen many times where people will create a name based on the current trend and the danger with that is when the trend goes away, so do you.

It's like you stamped yourself with an expiration date. The same could be said about tying your name to a location. It might imply it's the only customer base you serve. Then, if you start growing in the industry and branch out, that can also indicate outdated information sending a message to your audience that you are not current, completely limiting your potential.

Be sure not to make-up odd words, spellings or create acronyms that can really damage your brand image. Keep in mind, your brand has a little over five seconds to make an impression. When people are emotionally connected with a brand value, they are likely to build loyalty to a business after a great experience with their initial purchase.

But it starts with that first impression. It takes several exposures to your business name and brand to start creating awareness that you exist… so you want to be unforgettable. Taking these extra steps to stand out will help to eliminate confusion as to what and who you are, allowing for the A.I. search bots to find you easily and open doors to new followers.

This leads us to the next step… ***CREATE A LOGO THAT BEST REPRESENTS YOU VISUALLY.***

Although your company name will have a distinct identity that will project who you are and what you do, your logo reinforces the brand image as to how others perceive you.

Now once again, even if you didn't have a storefront, imagine what it would look like if you did and how you would sum it up in a company logo.

LET'S ENVISION WHAT YOUR STORE FRONT LOOKS LIKE: "What is the color theme of what you are envisioning?" "How are you represented: modern, trendy, classic, ultra professional, very business-like, laid back, casual, funny, quirky. Be very careful that you're certain of the company name and logo! Once you launch with that, people who find you may not be ready to consult with you or buy immediately, but they will hold on to your information for a while. I have seen people lose prospects, customers, and clients to other companies because of name and/or logo changes that are no longer recognizable.

WHAT YOU'RE BUILDING IN YOUR INDUSTRY IS TRUST AND LONGEVITY. YOU WANT PEOPLE YOU'VE REACHED OUT TO, TO REMEMBER YOU FOR A LIFETIME AND CAN ALWAYS FIND YOU.

The reality is not everyone is potential. They might not be interested at the moment in buying in on your offer. As a matter of fact, they usually aren't, and so sometimes you may have to drip on them several times for them to see the potential to what you are offering.

So, if you go missing or you stop posting, it stops that dripping process altogether. So just remember that if you come across a "NO" doesn't really mean a "NO." It just means "Not now" but we drip on them with education materials to their pain points and eventually if it makes sense to them, you will have your buyer. The longer you have the same company name and logo, the better you are found. Most companies might go through one concept or logo change and usually, it's to bring on a better image. So, you have to be careful with that. You should be 100% sure of your final design because you don't want to confuse your target audience by changing it too many times. It can create a bad taste or mistrust in your consumer.

Now, let's talk about your brand purpose, your promise, your values; what identifies you and how you differ from your competition, and your brand positioning in the marketplace.

It's what I call the **MISSION STATEMENT.** Once again, it is one of the core elements of your brand identity that aligns with the foundation of the company. It's the culture and the standard you strive for and aim for as a whole team.

Crafting a mission statement may feel a little overwhelming, especially if you just threw ideas up against the wall in hopes that something sticks, because - as mentioned earlier - you may have just started by putting the cart before the horse and not having your business plan properly launched and in place. So here are some things to remember when writing a mission statement. Outline what problem your company's product, service, and/or opportunity can solve.

"Why does your company exist?"

"How does your company operate and what sets you apart from your competition?"

"Highlight your company's purpose, promise and values and why customers should buy from you."

Here are a few examples to give you an idea:

Here's mine, for instance: **"JENNIFER WELCH"**

Empowering entrepreneurs to build an authentic and successful online presence that sets you apart from your competition, creating financial security that YOU own. My purpose and commitment as a brand strategist, digital marketer, blogger, web designer, global trainer and recruiter is to position you in the marketplace to maximize marketing efforts, generate leads, and increase income without sacrificing time.

My Tagline - **"Build a BRAND New You!"**

BUILD A
BRAND
NEW YOU!

You will notice that I have a tag line as well - "Build a BRAND New You," which is the last thing that you need to finalize your foundation as a business.

Here is another example:

A high-end business clothing store:

"JenSwag" Affordable and stylish men's and women's clothing line that fits the everyday entrepreneur from daywear to evening wear. Our commitment is to provide only the best styles and sophistication, to create a professional and positive impact and lift your status in your community.

The Tagline - *"Where chic meets sleek"*

These are just a few examples to help you craft the best mission statement that totally represents your core values and how your brand will fit your industry. You will need a very strong tagline that is brief, yet descriptive and easy to remember that aligns itself with your whole brand identity.

We want to create continuity and so no matter how cool your tagline may be, if it doesn't make sense to your brand, you may confuse and lose your audience altogether. So be mindful of that. This tagline can be helpful in your bio on social media, website header, email signature and much more.

SO, LET'S QUICKLY RECAP...

Once you build your brand identity, the name of your company that represents who you are and what you do, your logo that reinforces your brand image, a mission statement and a tagline that sums up your brand identity, this is where your company will start to come to life. I can promise at this point, you can start standing tall because now, when you are talking with people and sharing your product, service, or opportunity, you can feel good knowing that you can stand behind a company name that has purpose and meaning that will help drive your sales home. It's one thing to work for a company and stand behind its name, but it's a greater feeling when it's your own.

You can feel proud to go out and share what you know is absolutely yours. YOU OWN IT!! The chances of you working harder for your own success are higher than working for someone else to make them successful.

IT ISN'T UNTIL YOU ARE EXTREMELY
UNCOMFORTABLE THAT YOU WILL NOTICE
POSITIVE CHANGE TAKING PLACE AND
MAJOR GROWTH STARTING TO MANIFEST IN
YOUR BUSINESS.

Once again, we still need to make sure we tighten it up
a bit and make sure that the foundation you've created
will hold up by adding disciplined structures to your
business. Your name means nothing if there is no
sustainability when trying to make sure that your daily
operations run smoothly and without any hiccups.

This is a critical step for the customer to TRUST you
and feel good about what they are getting involved
with. It will help eliminate any questions on how you
run your establishment and is the difference maker to
customer retention and longevity.

For some of you who may already have an existing
company with your branding in place, change can be
difficult. Be careful when creating your brand package,
because when changing your brand, you don't want to
lose clients or customers in the process. If your
business has been struggling, it could have something
to do with your brand. So, if you have not had any
activity in a while, then revisiting this might be a good

Build a **BRAND** New You!

idea to make the shift in a direction that your business can thrive and then stick with it.

So, yes, change can be difficult, but sometimes change is needed in order to receive major increase and growth!

THE WAY YOU RESPOND TO CHANGE IS WHAT WILL DIFFERENTIATE YOU FROM THOSE WHO FEAR THE UNKNOWN AND DEFINES YOUR JOURNEY.

Sometimes, it takes a major shift in order to keep you from becoming stale or irrelevant. Your customers and prospects are looking for new and innovative products and opportunities. It's once again, "What separates you from all the rest." If you're part of a successful company, other companies want to emulate what you do in order to emulate your success.

It's the mark of a good company to have others try to copy you. Once your competitors have imitated you, how are you any better than them? How are you going to attract people to your opportunity (or product or service) instead of theirs? Just like our cell phones, and computers, etc. technology will eventually force us to change whether we like it or not. Kind of how we need to be with our business, right?

Part of what is going to set us apart is going the distance and constantly being ahead of your competitors and always being one step ahead. If you are not on top of building your business to what is current and relevant today and learn to take risks from time to time to better your business, you will always be chasing work down and working for someone who does. Taking risks is nothing. We do it to ourselves every day. When we don't try or make a move, that is a risk!

Humans, by nature, are creatures of habit. We like things that we can repeat. It helps us move faster when those movements are automatic and gives us a great sense of comfort when we can do things without even thinking about it. So, why not adapt and be good at the things that will make us better people and turn them into valuable habits? Bottomline... your desire for success, will be the determining factor to incorporating positive habits in your life that will help you reach your potential and push you to new heights.

YOU HAVE TO BE INNOVATIVE TO KEEP UP WITH THE CURRENT TIMES. OTHER-WISE, YOU WILL BE LEFT BEHIND FORCED INTO DOING IT ANYWAY LATER. SO, YOU MIGHT AS WELL START NOW!

YOU HAVE TWO CHOICES

You can whine about how you really liked the original brand. Many people do that. What ends up happening is that they never find new people to talk to, or worse yet, they drive away the people they were talking to.

Their business goes nowhere, they grow stale and bitter. They never recover their investment in their business and wonder how everyone else is having success and what special thing they did or trait they possessed to make money. Or you can reset yourself.

Forget about what was and look for the benefits in what's coming – the new branding package, new look, the new approach – and RUN WITH IT. Put forth the same effort into the new as you did with the old. You have an opportunity to be one of the best out of the gates, just by making these simple steps and mindset shift. It is those people who see the greatest reward.

As the saying goes, "Some people make things happen, some watch what happens, and others wonder what happened." Do you want to watch others or be the one who is making things happen? Companies have to change and innovate. We can't control how or when. All we can do is accept that the change is happening and embrace it with excitement.

The more excited you are about change; the more people will see that in you, and they will gravitate toward you. At the end of the day, your product, service, or opportunity is not what you sell; it's in fact - **YOU**.

Have you ever heard that saying, "if you catch on fire, people from miles away will come watch you burn". I can remember a moment when I was in school in my younger years, if a fight broke out, you knew it because people would run over to get a front row view, because people in general are nosy and curious. So, let's give people something to talk about. You owe it to yourself, your team, and your clients or customers to see those small changes through. It's important that you keep the core of your company in intact, maintaining high regards with integrity, values, and leadership.

IF YOU SHOW YOU HAVE ENTHUSIASM AND CONFIDENCE IN WHO YOU ARE, IT REALLY DOESN'T MATTER WHAT THE COMPANY CHANGES ARE, PEOPLE ARE LOOKING TO WORK WITH YOU. PEOPLE WILL FOLLOW YOU BECAUSE YOU'RE CONSISTENT EVEN IN THE FACE OF CHANGE.

CHAPTERTHREE

BUILD A STRUCTURE
AROUND YOUR BUSINESS

Building a strong structure around your business is just as important as building your brand identity. They work hand in hand. As mentioned earlier, part of why we don't get our consumers is that we don't even know why we are even doing what we are doing half the time, and our clients see right through that. Some of you just jumped in and don't even have a clue or have YOUR structure in place with business concepts that you should follow.

It's like having a flea market event at the last minute. You threw items in the car, leaving you guessing later what you're selling, the cost of what you are selling or even if the item you are selling is something that makes sense to sell at a flea market and you are caught off guard when people are coming at you asking you questions. You have to learn your environment and how to cater that product to the masses. Instead, your items just sit there, because they do not belong in that environment, and nobody has any interest, because they figured since you must not know much about it or care to then it's not that big of a deal for them to be interested in it. Now that we have accomplished who you are and you're starting to look like a real company with your company name and what you stand for, people will start taking you more seriously, can now trust you, and see your value. In this chapter, I am going to cover some basic structure in business to help set you up completely and compliment the foundation you've created necessary for you to fully launch the daily operational part of your business so you can work effectively and be proud of how you function on a daily basis. This should give you every reason why you would want to get up every morning and do what you love to do because you don't feel overwhelmed or unaware. It all starts with getting your life in order so that you can feel good about your business operating at full capacity. It is important to BE ORGANIZED.

YOUR BUSINESS IS COUNTING ON IT!

MOST FEAR OF FAILURE IS ROOTED IN THE UNKNOWN. KNOWING IS HALF THE BATTLE, SO IT IS IMPORTANT TO BE INTENTIONAL, AND GO OUT OF YOUR WAY TO ALWAYS LEARN. BE IN THE KNOW!

Some people call this step 'setting up office.' You want to do this quickly and move on. This is to be done during downtime, not during money-making time. The whole point of it is to allow you to function in the most efficient manner and to reduce a few mistakes that cause people to miss appointments, contacts or follow-ups.

Have a designated workplace that is free from distraction, in which to make calls and conduct your business. The reality is without this, we can really feel out of sorts, not in the game, put off, and unreliable to your business.

Always leave your work area clean and all papers filed away when you finish working. Being organized will help you get through the day by finding things easier and getting through them quickly.

This leads me to discuss speed in your business. Being quick and on your toes is VERY IMPORTANT. Learn urgency... have a "do it now" attitude! Avoid procrastination, with the exception of tasks that are unimportant to your business. One of the best ways to learn and to keep urgency in the forefront is to always plan and be a few steps ahead. Be aware of this and be on top of it so that it doesn't hold you back or miss out on opportunities. Having a business journal, log chart or appointment book is handy in keeping organized. With that, pick the start of your work week the evening prior, plan the upcoming week's activities and goals, and write them in a week at a glance appointment book.

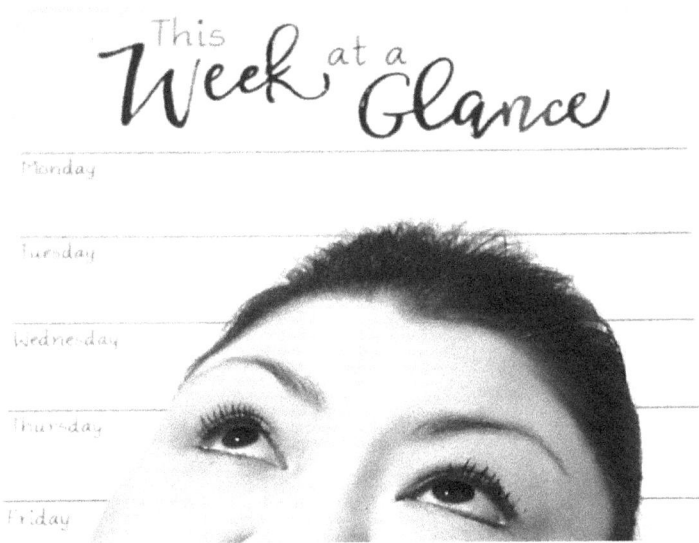

If my week starts on a Monday, I will prepare my week in advance the night before. So, in this case it would be Sunday. I know that with today's technology and how everything has an app, or how everything is moving online, everyone likes to use their mobile calendars for their appointments. I find that having a mobile calendar is great but could have the potential to have electronic errors like missed appointments or missed opportunities because it isn't in your face, or you turned your phone to silent and didn't hear the alarm, or a call came through and distracted you. I would highly recommend HAVING A PHYSICAL APPOINTMENT BOOK ON HAND, one with a week at a glance, to be exact, as backup.

There are so many reasons to make sure you have a paper back up. It prevents mishaps that can upset your customers or prospects because customer service is key to having a great customer experience. Most people operate on a weekly or monthly basis. A weekly planner allows you to see a bigger picture but gives you enough space to write in details. Look for one with timeslots that are conducive to when you work your business. Customer Service is a hallmark of a good business. In fact, it is the number one key in building relationships online

CUSTOMER
FRIENDLY
SUPPORTIVE
MOTIVATED
POSITIVE
SOCIALABLE
RESPECTFUL

through your social media presence. Now, it doesn't mean that the customer is always right; but the bottom line is that, in the end, they are the customer. Customer service means so much in many different ways.

Your attitude and how you handle things could be a make it or break it for the retention of your business. So here are a few small details to improve the customer service dynamics with your prospects and people in and around your office and workplace. Don't speak negativity, stay positive, and leave politics, drama, and religion out of your conversations.

There is a time and place for those things, and you do not want to skew your prospects or business associates to react to your beliefs.

You may stand for something or have strong opinions, but remember, we are to provide our customers with solutions to their problems first and foremost.

Customer Service is also about providing the utmost attention to your prospect, client, or partner. Know your cell phone etiquette! It needs to be OFF/SILENT and put away when you are in training, meetings, or events with a prospective client. Both parties need your undivided attention. Make sure you have a professional voicemail greeting on your cell phone.

When answering your business line, be sure to answer it professionally: *"Hello, this is Jennifer..."*

Sometimes, investing in a good hands-free headset can help set you up for better posture when you speak with people. People can hear when you are straining to hold your phone.

Your body language sets the tone of your voice. It also frees your hand to write notes and be on top of the needs of your prospects, clients and/or customers. Follow up is the key!! Return all calls within 24 hours. When you have a habit of not getting back to people promptly, it can annoy people and drive them to do business with others instead. Follow up will prevent you from losing a number or forgetting why someone called.

Also, be sure to check your caller ID log on your business line or cell phone so that you can call back people who don't leave a message. When doing this, write those numbers down in your call log for easy reference. DO NOT rely on scrolling back through your phone to find someone's number. Give every possible way people can reach you so that you don't lose business. Be prompt and deliver on your promise to get back when you say you will. INTEGRITY IS BIG! If you are busy, be sure to have lines of communication indicating that.

COMMUNICATION IS KEY!! This leads me to an important aspect of business and that is MANAGING YOUR TIME.

THERE IS NO SUCH THING AS –

"TIME MANAGEMENT!!" We all have the same 24 hours in a day – every day.

What you can do is manage your priorities to be the most effective with the time you have. At the end of the workday, ask yourself, "If I had someone on my payroll and they did exactly what I did today, would I keep them?"

Be careful how much non-income producing time you spend on the phone with someone. Plan your work and work your plan. Set your hours of operation. Develop a time schedule in which to build your business and adhere to it. Mark this time in your appointment book and have it open every day as a reminder. Having a full calendar is a great sign. You will be able to physically see the activities happening needed to accomplish set goals for that week. Don't fool yourself, you need to Know the difference between busy and productive. If it's not income producing, you don't have time for it, period!

Refer to your APPOINTMENT BOOK 'DAILY.' As I mentioned earlier, this weekly planner will allow you to visualize your week right in front of you. It allows you to be organized and provides you with daily accountability that you need to stay on task and schedule important tasks at the time of the day when you are at your best.

Calls to partners need to be done during down time. Some people who pick up a side gig may only have a few hours a day to commit to making money. Why would you spend that time training or talking on how you will do it? That will not produce income. So always remember to set up time for that during your downtime and not during income producing hours. Be bold and let your team members know this ahead of time.

Confirm all appointments! You only have one real commodity and that is your time. Don't waste it by getting stood up on your appointments. Confirming appointments also conveys that you are a professional and your time is valuable just as much as your customer's.

Practice short-term massive action. If you want your business to grow quickly, follow the process that most owners follow. Whether you are an entrepreneur, a busy professional, or a storefront owner, creating a system that organizes your day will allow you to spend less time worrying or planning on what to do next and get the job completed. It's funny to think how we tend to complicate the process even when we know what has to be done. It's like asking a child to clean his room; a very simple process, right? But they agonize over the steps in which they need to accomplish the end result even though they have done it before. Yes, it's simple but it may not be easy. We build mental roadblocks and justification for not starting because we can't get past the enormity of the overall task. It is crucial to have a simple step-by-step process, a system that becomes the core of your daily income producing activities. This process can be implemented in all types of businesses no matter the industry, leveraging your time in the best way possible to gain new business and grow it.

Follow this *"FIVE STEP MASSIVE ACTION PLAN"* - the core principles to grow your business at any level. Know it, repeat it and live it! Let's go over the steps:

1. Build your network ... and grow your reach.

2. Set up appointments ... fill your calendar.

3. Do presentations ... you should be doing quite a few a day depending on your industry.

4. Follow up and close ... Know your call-to-action approach. Be bold and go in for the sale. Half the time your customer feeds off your direction. Go in for the close.

5. Training and personal development... always read a good book. Feed the mind and be serious about your business and stay plugged in!

If what you're doing doesn't fit into one of these five steps within your weekly appointment planner, then you are not making money on it and you should not be focusing on it but during down time. Add other activities only AFTER you've completed all your money-making activities.

THIS MAY SEEM VERY DIFFICULT BUT DO THE TASKS THAT YOU FEAR MOST AND ARE THE HARDEST FIRST. GET IT OUT OF THE WAY!

They are usually the more important things that you should be doing; keep working on them until completed. After that, everything else will seem easy and seamless. Learn to use the most important word in time management - "NO" - when people make demands on your time, for unimportant, low-priority or non-producing income tasks. Since time is limited/valuable, every time you say "YES" to one thing, you are saying "NO" to something else.

One thing that can short-circuit your journey into owning your own business and the freedom it offers is a lack of direction. It's also one of the things I'm constantly helping people to define. Setting a goal provides a compass of where you want to go. While achieving that goal, you can feel so much more satisfied than 'accidentally' getting there. It drives us and pushes us forward.

TIPS ON HOW TO SET GOALS IN YOUR BUSINESS: Write down your goals. Place it where they can be viewed. Think about what you're going for and how you're going to get there. This is going to help you define what you're shooting for, your end result, and your reward in the end. It's not enough to say, "I want to be successful." It needs to be specific, or it's not a goal. For example: "I want to impact ___ number of lives in ___ number of days" and go for it. Define your GOALS and monthly business budget to accomplish these goals. Have a business budget ledger. This will help you monitor the money you are spending and the profit you should be making every month. When you invest, there should always be an ROI (Return on Investment). If you do not see the return, don't invest in that anymore.

THE BIGGEST SECRET TO SUCCESS IN ANY GREAT AND PROFITABLE BUSINESS IS SPEED. LEARNING URGENCY IS KEY.

It is very important to dedicate yourself to your goal and go for it. When you start, have the end date in mind. The question after you start is, are you going to keep moving? People often say, "I'll start my diet on Monday," and then they keep starting and starting but never finishing. Plant your stake in the ground at the starting point and never look back. Just keep that end date in front of you. When you set the start and end date, it's good to have a calendar, accountability log, whiteboard, vision board, etc., to put the dates in front of you that you can see on a daily basis. This will help keep you mentally accountable. Decide what you're going for. It could be a company contest, a promotion, or a new level of income. Maybe even a raise.

The most important thing is to focus on one goal at a time and run. When you do this, be sure to sit with your family and commit to that goal. Let them know how hitting your goal is going to benefit the whole family, get them involved, and make it fun! When the family is involved in holding you accountable, it makes the process that much easier to accomplish as they are pushing and encouraging you to keep going.

In the end, you may be surprised how much support and help you may get when you truly sit down and involve your family. Include them in your reward, like a family vacation, where they, too, have something to gain from it to help you get to your goal. In order to reach your main goal, you need to break it down into smaller, actionable pieces. Do the math. Network marketing businesses or sales companies are driven by productivity; therefore, most promotions and incentives are tied to that. If your incentive is to have a certain number of new team members, or a quota you are trying to meet, you need to figure out how many presentations it will take, how many follow-ups, etc. Break it down, and you will stay on track.

Likewise, if your promotion is based on acquiring a specific volume of business, you will need to assess and add up how many team members it takes, how many customers, how much your team is adding to that number, and so on. You need to be specific and tangible. You're not recruiting a number or a dollar sign, you're recruiting and helping people. Always strive for more and do better.

Put yourself on a per day goal. Set up a whiteboard, or better yet, two whiteboards. One will be a calendar board with your plan. The other is a board for your dreams and goals. Maybe a vacation, a car, or a house, etc. Focus is really important here. If there are a couple of incentive opportunities, but they don't align with each other, or your primary goal isn't going to help you win, choose which it is that you are going for and stick to it. If you can get laser-focused then your goal is very much within reach.

FOCUS ON HELPING PEOPLE AND SERVING THEM AT THEIR NEEDS. THE MONEY WILL AUTOMATICALLY FOLLOW.

Be sure to share your goal with your team leader or management team; they will help you and keep you accountable. Also, you need to share your goal with your team. When your partners see you in action, it will motivate them to get into action for themselves and for YOU. They are another source of accountability and reward for accomplishing your goal as a whole.

Constantly build your network. You will learn in later chapters the different ways to get people chasing you down. It's all about having a list of prospective clients or customers constantly flowing into your funnel at all times. You never want your funnel to dry up.

You want to start that funnel with some people ready to contact on day one so that you're not waiting around, wasting precious time. Those people you've been meaning to follow up with are a good start for hitting the ground running right away. Or maybe those new contacts you've made recently. Get folks participating in your new launch. Referrals are another sure way to fill that funnel with qualified prospects.

Don't delay sharing your product, service, or opportunity; you want to get that wheel turning as soon as possible. The quicker you do, the easier it is to get it going and to keep it going.

This is where you take your plan of how many people it takes to hit your goal and work backwards to find out how many people you need to have on your list in order to end up with the correct number of people joining your company or signing up with you, or having people buy into your product, service or opportunity. It's about you putting your launch into action. Contact people, do your follow-ups, and schedule presentations. Keep your appointment book full and schedule a minimum of 3-5 appointments and/or presentations a day.

When your team sees you in activity and constantly on the move, so focused and plugged in, it will motivate them as well. Work is not setting up office or preparing your marketing. It's that infectious daily grit that pumps us up and becomes contagious. The only thing that counts here is income-producing activities: contacting people, following up, doing presentations, following up some more, and most importantly, having them join you or purchase.

So, again, it's not enough just to have a logo and brand identity. You have to have important structures in place to guarantee productivity. You might look at owning your own business as being difficult to start at first, but, if you think about it… the idea of working 40 hours for 40 years, only to retire on 40%... well, now that is difficult to swallow.

Just take it one day at a time, having bite size goals that build up to accomplish the bigger goals. You've heard the saying, "How do you eat a whole elephant? One bite at a time, silly!" Having your stuff together to me is less difficult moving forward than trying to put the cart before the horse and short cutting it, feeling stuck, overwhelmed, and stressed over a business you started that is not making any money.

What I love about what you have learned and what I have shared with you so far is that you are now standing from a position of strength and able to grow confidently in your field and boldly deliver what you offer.

Let's be honest here…

I always hear people say, "I'm not in it for the money", but don't kid yourself… I hate to say it, but money is right up there next to oxygen.

SO YES, **YOU'RE IN IT FOR THE MONEY!!**

The more you realize it, the greater your mindset and power to become even more will shift in that direction. We may have a passion for what we do and love it, but we do want to reap the benefits of all our hard work in the end. This can result in repeatable lifestyle income that can be carried on for generations to come, building a legitimate legacy for your family and loved ones.

Now, you should be getting a better understanding of your full potential and how you can effectively stand up to your competition with some of the ground work and structure of your business in place. People will start seeing that you are serious and mean business. Let's dive in deeper on how to become the authority in your industry and the expert where people will want to follow you and can't wait to follow you by treating your business like a real profitable entity and not a hobby, side gig or a small business. Start thinking bigger… **YOU ARE A BUSINESS, A LARGE SUCCESS!**

CHAPTERFOUR

BECOME THE EXPERT
PEOPLE WANT TO FOLLOW

The sky's the limit when it comes to online technology today and the opportunity to win and be very successful as an entrepreneur is endless!

The world is vast and constantly evolving right before our eyes. Technology is growing by leaps and bounds. It's growing so fast that when you purchase the latest tool, the next day, it's already outdated. The world is never stagnant when it comes to learning.

Our industry has moved into an era where people are making money teaching people new ideas. To think that we've gone from hotels to Airbnb's and from taxis to Ubers and Lyft's, is crazy!

So, to think that you can't be in business because your idea or concept could already be discovered, or that people will find it ridiculous, or that no one is looking for it… is so far from the truth. There is always someone teaching something about a new fad or idea as a paying side gig. WHY NOT??? This is kind of why *Shark Tank* is so popular. How many times have you come up with a cool gadget idea or concept, just later to discover that someone invented it already… ***"Shucks, right?"***

Man, to take that and turn it into something serious for greater financial growth and gains could be the ticket, right? Unfortunately, to know how to go about it and implement it is another story. We are creatures of habit, and I've learned that some people get put off if it's too much trouble. We tend to brush it off altogether. Somehow, we tell ourselves that it couldn't possibly happen to us.

But it's at that "ah-ha" moment that we ignore that God may be sending the blessing to become who you were always meant to be. Maybe you have to take extra steps. Maybe there is so much more to it that you need to implement. That is what separates the naysayers from the doers, which is key to becoming majorly successful. We worry not about 'what if we fail", but more about "if we don't try, what if?" It's all about taking risks and making that jump!

IT TAKES MAKING A SIMPLE DECISION – A POSITIVE MINDSHIFT FROM LOOKING AT A GLASS AS BEING HALF EMPTY TO HALF FULL

In today's world, if you can teach or show the "know-how" you can make money, bottom line! It's ever growing, and you have to have a positive and unshakable belief that it can be done and see yourself already there.

We are constantly searching online for answers to explain something or to teach us how to do it, how to use it, etc. We have even gone as far as incorporating A.I. technology to help with our everyday research. It has become the latest tool. It may seem as if it just keeps getting easier and easier to take the guesswork out of most things, but let's not forget, competition is getting bigger and bigger.

There is so much competition that it starts to play with our emotions, and we're not sure if we are even good enough to stand against our competitors. We second guess our truth, confidence, and capabilities because we feel that someone's talent might be better.

Sometimes, we go through what is called imposter syndrome, which refers to an internal struggle where you feel like you don't deserve your success, even though you worked very hard for it.

You see that you have genuine talents and that you are very good at what you do, but you start doubting it and you start feeling like a fake or a phony despite any success that you've achieved. I know how frustrating this could be and how it can hold us back even in areas that you have excelled in. I can only speak on this because we all go through a little bit of this. Good news, I am here to tell you that I got through it, and most of what you are going to learn in this book is how you can, too.

IMPOSTER SYNDROME

I remember attending a conference and receiving the best gift ever from one of my favorite mentors. It was presented in a small box, and I recall him saying "this gift is so unique and is the best thing you will ever receive." I thought, "WOW!! What could it possibly be?!" So, I quickly opened it, and to my surprise, I was taken aback a bit. It was simply a mirror.

At that time, I wasn't feeling good about myself, and I wasn't really looking my best. I was even having a bad hair day and thought – "Wow, great timing…" as I silently smirked. He proceeded to ask me to take a very good look at myself in the mirror, and he said, "God doesn't make mistakes. He made us all powerful and uniquely different for a purpose." At that moment, I still didn't get the point. I was more worried and too busy looking at my current flaws in the mirror than concentrating on his point! This can be true about how we can't stop looking at our past flaws that detract us from accomplishing the goal set before us.

In today's world we live in such an appearance-based society. People tend to be more concerned with how they look on camera than what they are actually doing to add value. We tend to lose sight of what people are really looking for. Nobody cares how you look; they just want to know you care. We never make the jump into putting our true selves out into the world for fear of what other people are thinking about us.

But the reality is in our fast-paced, crazy world of chaos, people gravitate to life changing stories and relatable content that brings the confidence we are looking for and lack. Impactful people don't care anymore how they look because they are more concerned about delivering a message that can help. Have you ever had a moment where you've lived vicariously through another person's experience? People today crave an experience, not just a product or a service. The trend now is to show more heart and authenticity.

If you want to survive in our industry don't disguise yourself but be true and transparent. I promise there will be people looking for YOU and your uniqueness who can identify with you. People today can sniff out a scam and they aren't afraid to say it like it is if they feel that person is not representing truthfully. Just be yourself.

Be real but exhibit empathy. Another good reason you shouldn't try so hard to be something you're not is that if your brand identity isn't consistent with your life story and testimonies, you will lose your audience's trust, all the while wondering who you are you trying to be. Don't be worried about how you look. Worry about getting your message and training across to the right person who needed to hear it. Again, in business, it's not about you; the focus is on your customer, your prospect, or your audience, and providing a solution to their needs. There are some people who will always find fault with what you do, even if you're right, and that's okay. Give them something to talk about. Isn't that essentially what we are trying to do; get their attention, create dialog, and engage? Once you've gotten their attention, turn it around and place the importance on them and how they will benefit. They will care more about what's in it for them than judging you. We are all running our own race. So, when it comes to it, there is no comparison. There is only one Xerox copy of you, and there will be a target audience for your presence.

Every leader who has risen to the top knows that they didn't have to invent new concepts in marketing. Some of your best leaders simply regurgitate, emulate, and repackage the same ideas from generations before them. You may be presenting the same information, but no one can duplicate your personality and character. That's what will attract like-minded people to you, those who are seeking something authentic.

Look at yourself in the mirror and ask yourself: "Would I join me?" or "Would I buy from me?" Some people are shocked with themselves when they come to the realization that there is a need for improvement.

That is the best place to start. Practice talking or doing a presentation in the mirror and critique yourself.

I did just that at the start of my business. I got so good at presenting in front of a mirror that I forgot I was talking to myself, and I was ready to join ME. As funny and as ridiculous as that may sound to present in front of a mirror to yourself, I can promise you, if there is anyone who is going to be the biggest critic is YOU.

As you get more comfortable, ask a friend if they could critique your presentation. Who knows? They just might see their potential and join you, too! Remember, in the meantime… as we're working our way up, continue working on yourself and mastering your craft to become the expert.

Because in the end, people will buy into the leader before they will buy into the vision. So, own it! Give them a reason they would want to follow you.

POPCORN IS PREPARED IN THE SAME POT, IN THE SAME HEAT, IN THE SAME OIL, BUT THE KERNELS DON'T POP AT THE SAME TIME. DON'T COMPARE YOURSELF TO OTHERS; YOUR TIME TO 'POP' IS COMING!! – UNKNOWN

So, you might be worried about becoming an "Imposter" and comparing yourself.

The truth is I would be more concerned about your delivery of your message to a client, prospect or customer sounding more like a robot with these new A.I. tools today, trying to be a copycat like everyone else, versus you just being yourself. The thought of how some people think today, how they can just pick up an idea or talent and share it on social media is mind boggling. But to think they are an authority is alarming, because are they? Are YOU? There is a huge difference between a hobby and a business.

Ask yourself - Is your authenticity and authority true and original to you? the secret is being authentic to you. there is far more value in being original and There is a tribe meant especially for YOU! just be patient!

SO, LET'S IDENTIFY THAT...

Sure, a hobby can still get you there with a few followers and maybe make a little money. However, whether your followers think you can lead them to success is another entity in itself. My biggest pet peeve is when I hear network marketers tell people that they do not have to know everything and their leaders or management team can handle it all, you know, that "passing the buck" or "it's not my job" mentality. What are you teaching or enabling, but that they will never know the true meaning of servitude or being a business owner, all the while, learning nothing about their niche. That kind of attitude gets them nowhere and they are treating their business like a hobby. In turn, the manager or the team leader is not learning either because their attitude is now, "I will do it myself," or basically becoming a one man show and the best thing going on their team. It's the "I can do it all" syndrome where they build it themselves and never really grow, just chasing their tail in a vicious cycle resulting in them quitting and creating a bad attitude - professional at everything and master of nothing. They've created a bad habit of thinking that they know everything because they've been through it but have not learned anything. Once again, they blame the company for why they worked so hard and why it just never worked out.

I believe that sometimes our "ALL IN" mentality means if our team doesn't do anything, we owe it to them to work their business because we don't want to let them down, and we take the brunt of their failures onto ourselves. I am here to say that is incorrect thinking and so far from the truth. In fact, you are setting yourself up for burnout and it is unsustainable and will not duplicate. If anything, it is self-sabotaging your growth. If you put the "ALL IN" mentality in your OWN business, those who partner with you will either want to learn from you because you paved the way and set the example for them, or… you may have to let them quit.

In the corporate world, you find the same problem, a manager having an ego and not being a team player. Did we not forget that our partners and employees are customers too? They also should receive the utmost customer service. When we don't give everyone the same opportunity to win, and we enable them to think what they want to hear instead of what they need to know to be great in this industry… then we have failed as business owners.

You want people to want to follow you because you set the example of how to do it, and then they follow suit and learn. Be brutally honest on educating them on the right information, from product education to being the best leader and mentor that they can be… **NOT THE BEST BOSS!**

WHEN PEOPLE CAN TRUST THE LEADERSHIP THAT IS WHEN THEY CAN SEE THE VISION. WHEN YOU PUT INTEGRITY AND CHARACTER AT THE FOREFRONT OF YOUR INTENTIONS, PEOPLE CAN'T HELP BUT TO FOLLOW.

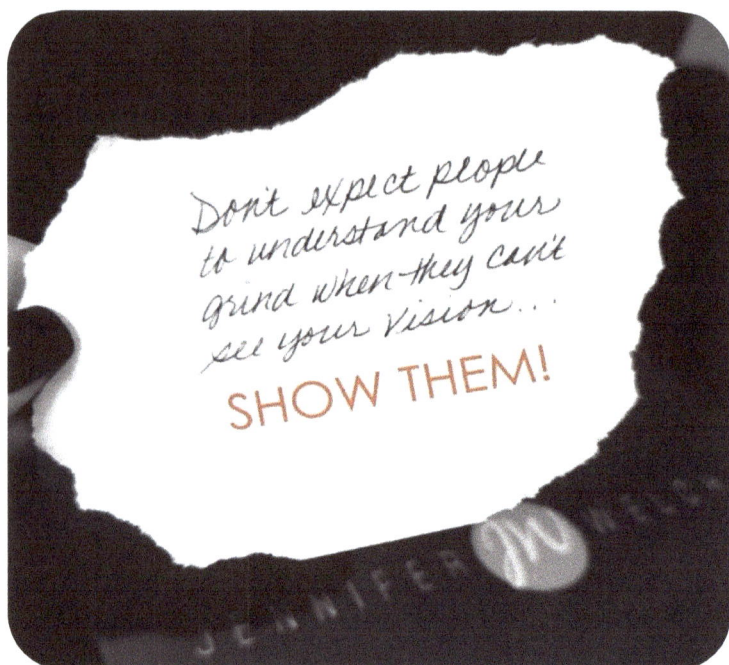

Don't expect people to understand your grind when they can't see your vision...

SHOW THEM!

WHAT DOES "ALL-IN" LOOK LIKE?

Building a business in network marketing requires you to be ALL IN. All-in isn't about working 24/7. Many people start their networking or home business on a very part-time basis. It's not how much time you spend, but your attitude and having a consistent process or system in place for your business or side hustle that is critical to your success. It doesn't happen by accident.

LET'S GET – "A. L. L. - I. N."

A - ACQUIRE CUSTOMERS AND BUSINESS PARTNERS

These are the basic tenets of network marketing, **getting everyone you know in the world on your product, service, or opportunity.** It's the foundation of businesses all over. Being consistent in your marketing and recruiting will solve all your business building problems. Being committed to growing your own business volume will promote you to be an example for the business partners you bring in to do the same.

L - LAUNCH YOUR CUSTOMERS AND BUSINESS PARTNERS

This is a big step that many network marketers miss. **Recruiting without a launching system means NOTHING in your business!**

WHAT YOU THINK ABOUT ON A DAILY BASIS BECOMES YOUR MAXIMUM POTENTIAL

Not launching your people is a big factor in contributing to that dreaded MLM graveyard. For example, in my health and wellness business, I provide my new business partners with a startup folder with tips and training right when they sign up, and I review it with them. It's a track to run on that they will duplicate with their team. I also go over their connection to the company; logging in on their business portal, setting up how to get paid, where to go for marketing and learning materials, account, etc. Lastly, I make communication a big deal. I contact them daily and set the expectation that they should contact me with any questions or challenges.

Urgency equals success; so, it is critical to get them running right away. We can't assume that just because someone signs up for your opportunity, they know what they're doing and will just take off without you. You owe it to yourself and to your new business partners to walk them through at least the first 30 days because, more often than not, they are either very new or they've built up some bad habits, and you need to guide them to a successful process so that your hustle, side gig or business opportunity doesn't become "just another thing" they tried and didn't work. Do you want to retire in ten years or in a couple of years? How do you launch a customer? Simply show them how to use your product or service. Make it easy and enjoyable for them. Show them how to log in to their customer account and how to change their settings, reorder products, and enhance their services. And lastly, check in on them and make yourself available to them to make sure they are getting everything they can. Build that relationship, and you'll have an endless stream of referrals.

L - LEAVE NEGATIVITY BEHIND

Negativity spreads like a disease. You're trying to grow your business. Growth is positive, and so you must be, too, to keep that momentum turning in the right direction. If somebody comes to you with a problem, don't feed into it or let it rent space in your head. Find an answer, or something positive and encouraging to take away. Continue to dedicate time each day to personal development by reading a book or listening to audio books.

I - INTENTIONAL THINKING

No matter what anyone says, it takes effort and a plan to grow your business. Many people start their own home businesses to change their financial outlook, to attain financial freedom. **You can make a little extra**

money without a plan but attaining that life-altering income takes work and intention. The business partners who join you also need to see your dogged determination. They will look at you and be inspired, following what you do.

Leadership isn't about managing but teaching and being an example for your team. We tend to worry about everyone else's activity when we're not busy; that's called "management mode." But, if we ourselves are active, our business partners see this and are more encouraged. Would you rather build a business full of people all intentionally working together toward the same goal, or a group of people scattered in different directions?

N - NEXT LEVEL... RANK UP PROMOTION

If you're not moving up in rank, then you're going nowhere. You need always to look ahead at your next challenge and go for it. Is it a pin level advancement? Is it a business expansion? A monetary milestone? A contest? If you're not going for something, neither will your team. When that happens, all progress stops. Just like a wheel, it is hard to get it to start moving, but when it moves, it becomes easier to keep going. Thus, keeping your eyes on the next level will keep you moving in your business. When you put these steps together, a consistent process of handling your day by sharing your product or service and opportunity, a commitment to start customers and business partners on the right foot, maintain a positive mindset, plan your success, and keep looking at your next achievement, you'll turn your business into a lifestyle that gives you financial and time freedom.

Repeat this process - stick to it - and stay plugged in. This is what is going to propel you as an expert in your field that will not only get you loyal customers but leaders who follow you to the ends of the earth. This will prove once again that just by being intentional with your business, people will see how serious you are about running a true business and not a hobby. Because what is being portrayed on social media is that anyone can have a business and share it, but are they treating it like a real, paying business that can last for decades?

REMEMBER, IF YOU ARE GOING TO TREAT YOUR BUSINESS LIKE A HOBBY OR YOU HAVE A HOBBY MENTALITY... YOU WILL GET HOBBY PAY.

That is what is going to set them apart from their competition. There is only a small margin of people who actually do it right. So, when I say **there is so much room at the top**... that is a very serious statement.

This leads to dissatisfaction and boredom, which eventually kills excitement. The next thing you know, you're picking up something else, and then you're wondering why your captive audience stopped following you or has become disinterested. You are all over the place, and you have confused them and now you cannot be trusted. To them, you have become a flight risk!

You never want to confuse your target audience or your tribe. Remember, we are creatures of habit, and some people stay comfortable where they are at. Have you noticed that when companies go through changes, they start losing some of their customers or employees?

So, you want to stay consistent with what your audience loved about you from the beginning. This is why it is important not to worry about what your neighbor is doing or what they think of you. Watch out as fear will set in at this point and cause you to start making changes because of someone else's input or personal opinion.

STAND BEHIND YOUR BRAND! THERE IS NOBODY QUITE LIKE YOU! BELIEVE IT AND OWN IT!

Let's get something clear... In order to become an authority in your field and dominate the industry, you have to remove the hobby mentality once and for all. Your mindset needs to shift gears altogether and have the utmost commitment and unshakeable belief in your business that you know and understand that you have something incredible to offer people that gets you moving and shooting for that end goal. If you are a person looking to build and operate a real legitimate business, your intention is to make a profit. So why do some of us treat our business like a hobby?

Let's get into network marketing for a minute, for those who have trouble gaining an understanding of what a side gig is. A hobby is something you do for fun, never intending to make any money. So, be honest with yourself is that what you went into business for?

Some people want to put in hobby hours and hope to receive a huge payout in this type of industry.

It is definitely not a get rich quick scheme - at least not any of the ones I have ever been a part of that have changed my life. It's simply illegal. Owning your own business requires dedication and hard work.

This is why I say even in the network marketing arena, there are perks just for getting involved. For example, receiving a 1099, that's recognized through the government as a legitimate business, and has major tax advantages available to us, which can be a huge financial gain. If there are tax benefits to enable you to invest in your business, why wouldn't you treat it as such? This is another great example of how people take their network marketing business for granted and treat it like a hobby. We can either take advantage of owning our own business as a traditional store front or in network marketing, where you don't have to worry about traditional overhead expenses. Either way, what makes you think that building either one is any different? It is still a business and still requires a solid foundation to start one. Both take hard work and determination.

It all boils down to knowing what you want, what you're going for and WHY, so that people can take you seriously and believe that you can be an expert and an authority in your field.

Nobody wants to associate themselves with someone who doesn't know where they are going or is unsure of their expertise. Someone who changes from one company to another, chasing the next best thing instead of sticking with one and getting the best training that they can implement to dominate their competitors, builds no loyalty or proficiency.

I would rather work hard on one thing and be good at that, than to be a part of several things. Looking at it from this perspective - a jack of all trades and master of none, well, it doesn't really send a good message to your target audience about you, except that you like to hop from one best thing to another, implying that you can't finish or see things through or that you are unreliable! Don't let anyone fool you. Running a business takes discipline and hard work, but the payout is well worth it. When you commit to your company and see it through and be the best in your field, that's where experts are found!

I AM NOT INTERESTED IN BECOMING A JACK OF ALL TRADES MASTER OF NOTHING AND NEITHER SHOULD YOU. NEVER QUIT! FINISH WHAT YOU START AND SEE IT TO THE END!

Everything has to fall in line with your purpose, and you must be intentional from start to finish. Most people fall apart here. I will tell you people can tell and will see your true intentions.

Remember, most people today have their guard and radar up to look for a reason to shut you down and prove you wrong or that you won't be there for them to the end. Building their trust, being intentional, and being genuine is key. Leaders are always one step ahead. **Just keep in mind, IT STARTS AND ENDS WITH YOU!**

When you have that down you will notice people want to join you because they trust that you will always lead them to victory, that you will always have their back and be there for them. Reliability gives your prospects and/or business partners one of the strongest reasons to want to join YOU. You may have a great product, service, or opportunity, but they can buy that anywhere or go somewhere else. Remember, others sell it too, but why buy from or join YOU?

Sometimes, as mentioned earlier, we get so excited about getting a company going that we end up putting the cart before the horse, starting the business, and never getting everything in place. Eventually, it will result in a lack of credibility, trust, professionalism, etc. Putting a little time into preparing the launch of your business plays a big part in how successful your business can be. This practice will make you that much more powerful. Not to say that you can't just go out there and start selling printed t-shirts; but, after a while, when the growth starts happening and you want to raise the bar, to level up and get your business aligned with your target audience, your growth and retention is in place.

You want people hunting you down instead of you scraping for clients. If you don't prepare, you will have a hard time getting out of the stagnation that can eventually stunt the growth of your business. Can you imagine how many people who own their own business offer what you've got? But what makes you better, different and more appealing? What helps you stand out and sets you apart? Going the extra mile to set up your business is what will set you apart from your competition.

HAVING RETURN CUSTOMERS WHO REALLY VALUE YOU AS A COMPANY IS KEY AND CAN BE YOUR BEST TOOL FOR NEW BUSINESS

Taking these extra steps in your business can mean the difference in your clients coming back and maintaining customer loyalty and retention. Most of the time, people think there is a lot you must do to start.

It begins with simple key elements that I have laid out so far for you and how to implement them. You will learn in the next chapters what will turn you from rock-bottom busy professional to a rockstar entrepreneur, attracting your loyal fans and family tribe on and offline who will stay true to you.

Everything today is driven by having an online presence. It is very important to think about having the necessary tools to launch your business right and effectively so that you are recognized as the real deal, the expert that many will want to follow. Before we can even talk about cutting the ribbon and opening your store front, it is so important that not only have we created your foundation, but have also set up a solid, disciplined structure to put you in a position to be successful and develop your whole self to move from ordinary to extraordinary. It's time to level up and be extraordinary! Be intentional and start creating the daily habits needed to succeed. Here are the five basic necessities to start leveling up and becoming the best version of yourself!

5 THINGS YOU NEED FOR ↓ NEXT LEVEL SUCCESS

1. Schedule Your Time 2. Immerse Yourself 3. Repetition 4. Implementation 5. Master It!	**TIME TO FLEX & SHOW OFF!** F ind your voice & GO LIVE! L earn & get good at your skill E nter a group - don't do it alone X periment - run for 90 days

HERE ARE JUST A FEW MORE IMPORTANT THINGS TO REMEMBER:

- DRESS THE PART – BE UNIQUE, BE DIFFERENT... BE PROFESSIONAL!

- Set up your hours of operation and stick to it!

- Never forget that the most important emotional need for people is to feel important. Always bear this in mind when dealing with people.

- Stay busy when building your business.

- Keep your funnel full. If you are busy, you tend to eliminate negative thoughts.

- Lead by example. Understand that whatever you do, good or bad, your people will do.

- You are who you hang around with. So be a part of something bigger than yourself and lead your people to that.

- Confront the tasks that frighten you the most. Challenge yourself that if someone else can do it, you can do it.

- Don't blame others - accept personal responsibility for the state of your business.

- If you are not growing, ask yourself "Have I done everything possible for my business to grow?" "Have I been in contact with my CEO or leader daily?" if you have one.

- Ask yourself – "What did I learn from this?" - After every experience, especially the bad experiences.

- Always have a hunger for learning something. Don't grow stale in your industry. Be ahead!

- Read or listen to audio books!! If you have a hard time with this, start by setting aside ten minutes in your appointment book to consciously read.

- Challenge yourself to increase your time spent reading each day until you reach 30 minutes a day or even more. Grabbing this book is already setting you up in the right direction to feed your success and to totally crush it in your field of knowledge.

- Become a "work in progress" - always be improving yourself and your business.

- Connect with successful people and attend seminars. Sharpen that axe!

- Be mindful of who you hang around with because you tend to become like them.

- Address the attitude: If you have an "I'll just try it out to see if it works" attitude, forget about it! Because one small challenge arises and you're ready to quit.

- So, will you be here when the going gets tough? Choose to win and don't allow negativity to rent space in your head.

- Be aware of opportunities around you to expose your business. There are always people who are clearly unhappy about their job, money, services, etc. and will complain openly to anyone who will listen.

- Develop the habit of asking people what they do. Now, you can offer them a role or new business opportunity.

- Never accept "NO" as a final answer. Timing is the key. Log them for a later contact. You never know; their circumstances could change in 90 days.

- Listen 80 percent of the time, talk 20 percent.

- Tell others what _they_ are interested in knowing, _not_ what you think they should hear.

- Keep your approach simple, "Can I share my heart with you?" - easy right? Who can say no?

- Go for a 90 Day promotional run and get your family involved in it, making sure you plug into your team lead and let them know what you're going for so that they can assist and hold you accountable.

CHAPTER FIVE

BUILD TRUST AND WIN RAVING FANS

At this point, you should be really excited, and your head must be spinning with all kinds of ideas. I don't know about you, but when I started learning all this and grasping the concept, it finally started to make sense and things were starting to come together. I started to get excited about the launch of my business, and the positive direction it was heading.

I felt like I actually had it together and was feeling like I was becoming somebody important in my business and that I had an offer that people truly wanted that was improving lives. It was a complete game changer to feel that I stood for something and that I had a purpose in this world, to now being able to stand from a position of strength, know who I am and what I was offering.

To educate and to be trusted was when I started LOVING what I do. I genuinely found my passion and really started enjoying the process. I couldn't wait to wake up and see who I could help or provide for. It is such a humbling and rewarding feeling when you can finally have a voice that people want to hear from that's impacting so many lives. Trust is the biggest commodity in our industry. Because if people trust you, trust your knowledge and education on the information provided about your product or services and you can handle objections, then, you're in business.

Your customers will be willing to buy from you because they trust YOU. Be sure to detail and know what your company offers - Product, Services or Opportunity. Make sure that you are providing your consumer marketing information that handles objections before you share. Not knowing your stuff can kill your business. Keep in mind that KNOWLEDGE IS KEY!

People in general are skeptical and will find every reason to talk themselves out of buying or joining you. They will be so quick to object your offer, and the question will always be "what's in it for me, why should I join you, and why do I need your product, service or opportunity?" Once again, what sets you apart from everyone else? See, even though earlier on when you jumped into business without a foundation, it may have worked for a moment, but eventually, you are faced with adversity from competition and consumer comparison to why yours is any better. So being knowledgeable with your business to answer questions and provide why YOU will be a game changer for them is important in your approach.

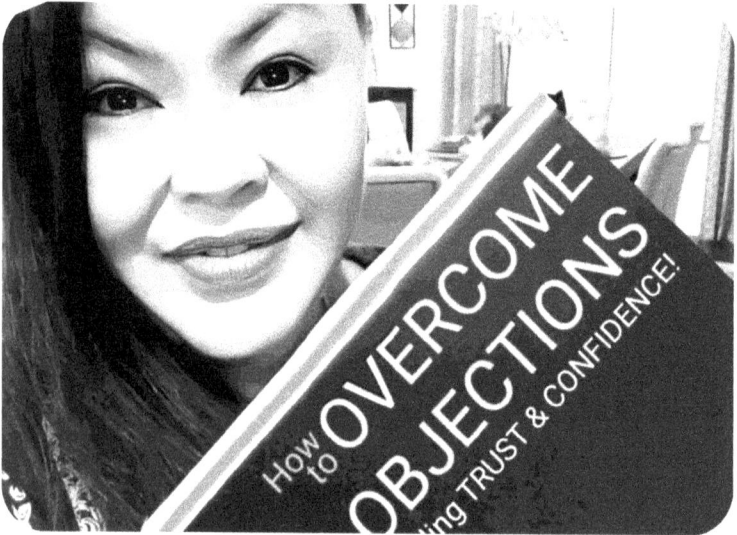

When you take your brick-and-mortar experience from the traditional sense to the internet, usually a lot of building your brand is already done because you can't open a store front without a name, right? Going into the social media scene, half the battle is already won because you have established your brand identity. Creating trust and building relationships is going to be more prevalent in your marketing efforts and content delivery. Being on social media may look very intimidating, especially since online marketing is huge today. But one thing you need to remember is that online marketing is no different than the days when we had the yellow page phone book. When you looked for "furniture store," you would get nothing but all the different furniture stores in your area with their contact info in the order in which those companies were willing to invest time and money to be found on the first page. The internet really isn't far from that concept. We just brought local traditional marketing to the internet and created tools that can position you at the top of your competition. What had us doing thousands of flyers in the past, or going door to door is so much simpler now with posting online and having millions of views. Having a higher visibility rate and a greater reach to that one post if done right can make a big difference in your marketing efforts online.

Once again, working smart, not hard I say. Using a few good hashtags that align with your content, more importantly keywords that people search for including alt tags and content behind our posts have become our flyer funnel, but we never have to leave our house to do it. This is why having a presence on social media is important. It is the surest and fastest way to grow.

Although offline local traditional marketing is still effective, the social media scene has dominated the online marketing world.

I always say that working smart, not hard, makes better sense with your time, especially if you are looking for a side gig that won't interfere with your current situation. Maybe you already have a job but need part time work, and you only have so much time in the day to make that income, or you can't work because you are a stay-at-home mom, then network marketing may be an attractive way for you to make money. Better reach and faster marketing with simple approaches, I call that winning!

As we go into the next chapters, to now brand yourself on social media, keep in mind, it's simply just taking your business and incorporating it online. That's it... there's no difference. You just want to create an online presence as if I just met you and I said, *"NICE TO MEET YOU."* How would that look online?

Whether you are doing online networking or taking your brick-and-mortar business to the internet, social media is going to allow you to open more doors to further your success and take marketing to a completely new level!

CHAPTER SIX

LAUNCH YOUR BUSINESS
ON SOCIA MEDIA

The next step now is to *CREATE YOUR BRAND ON MANY SOCIAL MEDIA PLATFORMS*.

Here is why it's important to build on social media…

Did you know in 2023 it was estimated that there are over 4 billion social media users worldwide. So, to think that we don't need social media to build our business is absurd.

Now, let me be clear on a few things before we dive right into it. It's important to understand that we don't close the door completely on local traditional marketing. Let's face it, I would not be here sharing this information with you if it wasn't for the local traditional marketing methods that I have led with so many years back and have paved the way for me today in bringing all that success as we know it to the internet.

We know it's all about numbers, working smart, not hard. So, taking your business to the internet has been very lucrative. It's the surest and fastest way to grow your business. Don't get me wrong, using the local traditional marketing way still works today. If someone comes within three feet of you, you would take that time to introduce yourself, right? So, the same can be said online. The only difference is we don't come in physical contact with anyone, making it that much easier to reach out to as many people by message versus face to face. If you are a business owner of any kind, even if you're a brick-and-mortar company that may be a service-driven business, I've found that local traditional marketing is becoming less and less productive and a thing of the past now that we have the internet. With today's technology and how things are vastly growing online, if you don't keep up with the times, your company can suffer a great deal from the lack of customer, client and prospect interactions. We are seeing more and more companies close up local shops and move their business to the internet to sell their products or services. Because the bottom line is, the way the world is functioning today, everyone is looking for an easier avenue to do things and they don't want to leave their homes. When it comes to businesses today, we've seen that most have shifted to online marketing to reach more people.

Being online, where most of your audience is, can be a complete game changer and can make a difference to the growth of your business. There are so many platforms to build your brand on. My advice is to get on as many as you possibly can that will deliver your brand, paying close attention to each platform, as each one delivers differently based on your target audience.

Just to break that down, here is what I've learned from working with some of the best social media platforms for growth. There are many others, but I just want to share a few of the benefits of the ones that I currently use. Keep in mind, the rules on these platforms as well as their algorithms can change at any time.

Let's start with:

FACEBOOK – It's a great resource for businesses today. You are able to get a larger diversified fan base with a greater and advanced target reach worldwide and more engagement tools and visibility through advertising on groups, multiple business pages, messenger, ad managers and leveraging the insights tool.

INSTAGRAM – Has been deemed the most popular choice for business growth, with its visual driven approach, which allows for storytelling through images, videos and stories that engage with your audience and build a fan base. It's a great way to also advertise your product and services through a digital storefront ecommerce business. You can utilize the tools on IG to gauge your performance with analytics that measure traffic metrics and allow you to adjust your strategies accordingly.

LINKEDIN – a go-to leading professional networking platform, where most professionals make connections that lead to opportunities. Great for B2B businesses to reach decision makers and thought leaders directly. Many recruiters use this avenue to pursue other professionals and talent. Leverage ads for targeted marketing campaigns.

TIK TOK – This platform is rapidly growing by leaps and bounds, gaining major popularity with the younger generation - Gen Z's. Very similar to Instagram, creating a visual story board using more small video clips from funny, edgy, and trendy to real life videos that instantly grab your attention. Users are able to showcase their products and services with a short commercial-like ad video without having to pay for costly TV advertisements. Able to piggyback on other successful trends, collaborations, and duet with them to move up and expand more on reach and credibility.

YOUTUBE – dominates video content. As mentioned before, people prefer easy; and videos are the most popular. Like reading books, for instance, people prefer to watch a video or listen to audio rather than reading to save on time or multitasking during busy times. So, the convenience and the engagement are higher on this platform. This is an excellent platform to stablish your brand through demos, tutorials, and vlogs. It is just as important when tying your website into SEO (Search Engine Optimization), an important element to launching your business visibility, is also to connect on YouTube. YouTube is the second largest search engine.

Interconnecting all of these social media platforms is important to how they co-exist with each other and how each one can play a major part in the growth of your business, if utilized correctly. When they all work complimentary with each other it can create a collective impact and a sure sign of getting yourself visibility and maximizing your online presence, thus creating an organic reach.

They all play a part in leading people to your offer, considering that you make sure that the content and videos are attractive and cohesive to who you are, providing a powerful hook that grabs the attention of your target audience.

Use your analytics to measure your metrics and use the insight tools to gauge how your content strategy is doing, and most importantly, create continuity to your brand and deliver a powerful message that converts to a call-to-action. You will craft a brand identity that keeps people wanting more and a long-term, sustainable presence and engagement.

So, it is very important to choose the right platform that will work best for your brand and, most importantly, determine who you're looking for and what your ideal target audience will look like. Content is key, so driving the right audience to your information is going to be very important, and you want to create unique content for each platform that caters to how that platform will deliver your message to its type of crowd.

Now, there is nothing that says you can't repurpose content from one platform to the other. Just be aware that when you do so, you are being intentional about it and that it makes sense to your target audience. You want to drive continuity.

Not all platforms are created equally. Each is unique to its users' behavior, culture, and content formats. So, it is crucial to tailor your content to suit each platform and target audience. Be sure you know and can identify what your audience is looking for and then focus on being consistent, because consistency breeds familiarity, familiarity breeds trust.

Trust is the most important attribute in strengthening relationships and gaining raving fans on social media. This will give you every possible reach to effectively grow your business. Let's set up and update your brand image on your social media platforms to reflect congruency and give it a cool makeover. If you are wondering where to start, start with the social media you are on the most and then branch off from there. We want to make sure that your brand image matches your brand identity and position your brand properly in the marketplace.

Be sure to start by having a clear, fun and good quality picture of yourself. Make sure that picture is being used as your profile picture and nothing else. When they land on one of your social media platforms and they check your profile and see your picture, it's as if you're saying, *"HI THERE! NICE TO MEET YOU!"*

If you do not provide a personal picture of yourself, it's sending several bad messages like – "Is this a real person or company that can be trusted?" Or "how can I follow a leader who won't show his face and is not present or is constantly hiding?" So, be sure to get nice pictures done of yourself. With A.I. or new cell phone camera technology, you can create nice professional filtered pictures to represent your company, not those outlandish A.I. pictures that look nothing like you, of course, so be cautious and tasteful. If you can do that, it sure does save time and money rather than sitting through a photo shoot. On social media make sure your profile picture is updated, banner has continuity to you and your business lifestyle, and your bio is a quick description of what you offer using search terms that will stand out and be found on Google.

This allows people to see there are real people who they will be dealing with, giving your company credibility and trust. Because remember, when you are offering your product or services, you are not really selling them, you are selling YOU first.

AT THIS POINT, YOU'RE PROBABLY STILL SCRATCHING YOUR HEAD WHEN IT COMES TO FIGURING OUT WHAT TO SAY OR HOW TO START ON SOCIAL MEDIA. AS YOU READ ON, IT WILL START TO MAKE SENSE.

Keeping track of posting, commenting, liking, and following can be challenging in itself, in addition to coming up with different topics on a regular basis to attract the kind of audience you're looking for. So having a daily routine that keeps you organized can help with bringing those engagements. I cannot say enough how important it is to keep up with today's industry. I urge you to learn anything and everything that can help lead you to more prospects. Remember, growth takes place during stages of being uncomfortable. I understand that it may feel overwhelming at first. Social media is a beast in itself to get into marketing; but it is so worth it once you get the concept down. If you plan to build a solid business as well as a team of leaders, it's good to be diverse in your marketing efforts. Before we start, I know your head is spinning with lots of questions and wondering:

"What social media platforms should I be on?"

"Which platform is best for my business?"

"Can I put my company logo as my profile pic?"

"Do I need a separate business account?"

"Can I share same content on all platforms?"

"Do I need so many friends for this to work?

"How do I gain followers?"

No worries... Let's start with the platform you're more established on and more familiar with, shall we? And we will cover these questions through the next chapters. It will be easier to gain momentum of course if you already have friends or followers, and you should already know the basics, like how to like, comment or reply, how to post, etc. As well as understanding the difference between your **timeline profile page** where you see just the photos and videos you personally posted that is only accessible by you and the **news feed page** that is a public place, an open forum where we use to connect to one another by messaging, commenting, posts pictures, videos, sharing our stories and milestones, etc. If you're already on a few platforms, as mentioned earlier, make it easy on yourself by refurbishing past content and stories that can easily be shared again from one platform to another, so that you don't have to come up with something different each time. Just remember, each platform caters to a specific kind of crowd, and you will need to pay attention to the kind of message that you convey. You don't want to share videos or posts with watermarks on them from other platforms, as it could hurt your algorithms.

But it is a good idea to be on several platforms, for

higher visibility and reach for exponential growth. As I mentioned earlier, I find myself scratching my head for ideas on topics, but I just don't know where to begin. I was having a hard time grasping the concept and I was struggling with it early on in my career in the industry when social media was first introduced to me. **So, I get it! Been there, done that.**

One thing I started realizing is that if you go into this with just posting to be posting and not really sharing what's on your heart, even from an educational place with your intentions, your hopes to get through to somebody will be a waste of your time and your marketing efforts will suffer, not to mention that it could hurt your chances for the platforms to know your real intentions. It could close doors and opportunities for you. So, you will hear me often mention in this book about being intentional. Market to their heart instead of their head.

Because let's face it, we buy with emotions backed by logic. As we launch you into social media, having a **"weekly daily post topics"** cheat sheet on hand has been instrumental and can help a great deal with your posting.

Monday

MOTIVATIONAL MONDAY
MINDFUL MONDAY
MONDAY MORNING
MONDAY MEMORIES
MONDAY MOOD
MONDAY MADNESS
MAGIC MONDAY
MONDAY MINUTE
MENTORSHIP MONDAY

Tuesday

TIP TUESDAY
TRIP TUESDAY
TECH TUESDAY
TRANSFORMATION TUESDAY
TUESDAY TRAINING
TUNE-UP TUESDAY
TUESDAY TREAT
TESTIMONY TUESDAY
TRENDY TUESDAY
TUESDAY TOPIC

Wednesday

WELLNESS WEDNESDAY
WORKOUT WEDNESDAY
WEDNESDAY WORDS
WEDNESDAY WALK
WEDNESDAY WISDOM
WINNING WEDNESDAY
WINE WEDNESDAY
WARRIOR WEDNESDAY
WACKY WEDNESDAY
WORKDAY WEDNESDAY

Thursday

TRUTH THURSDAY
THROWBACK THURSDAY
THOUGHT THURSDAY
THIRSTY THURSDAY
THURSDAY TRAVEL
THURSDAY TEAMWORK
THURSDAY TRIVIA
THURSDAY TAKEAWAY
THANKFUL THURSDAY
THURSDAY TIPS

Friday

FIT FRIDAY
FRIDAY FUN DAY
FAMILY FRIDAY
FOLLOW-UP FRIDAY
FLASHBACK FRIDAY
FRIDAY FLICKS
FRIDAY FEELINGS
FEARLESS FRIDAY
FAB FRIDAY
TGIF

Saturday

SELFIE SATURDAY
SOCIAL SATURDAY
SATURDAY SWAG
SATURDAY SALES
SHOUTOUT SATURDAY
SATURDAY SHENANIGANS
SILLY SATURDAY
SATURDAY STYLE
SATURDAY SHOPPING
SATURDAY SPECIALS

Sunday

SUNDAY SERVICE
SCRIPTURE SUNDAY
START-UP SUNDAY
SPOTLIGHT SUNDAY
SUNDAY SWEAT
SOCIAL MEDIA SUNDAY
SUNDAY SESSION
SUNDAY SNUGGLES
SUNDAY SABBATICAL
SPA SUNDAY

WEEKLY DAILY POST TOPICS

Pick One Per Day
9 Weeks Worth

It has helped me to come up with great ideas that keep me from growing stale. Here are some topics for your social media posts that you can build content around for each day.

If you noticed, these daily ideas can also be included in your hashtags for that post. A **Hashtag** is a keyword that is prefaced by the hash symbol/pound sign-#. Hashtags are widely used on social media platforms as a form of user - generated tagging that enables cross referencing of content sharing a subject or theme.

I like to compare it to doing flyers from a local traditional sense but taking to the internet with a greater reach. Imagine some hashtags having a million followers, that's crazy! Working smart, not hard, I say! Just add a few (3-5) good ones that align with your content. Just be sure to use only one of these hashtags on your post, not the whole list! The list is designed to give you one topic per day, just choose one that suits you that day, but do not reuse the same content throughout the week.

Be creative, mix it up, and add your style and flare, keeping true to who you are, but making sure the content you deliver will convert to a call-to-action every time.

One big takeaway that I want you to get out of this is that if you follow this guide, you can put together a great plan to get your business marketing really up and running (and really growing) just with some consistent effort. Keep using this week at a glance - daily social media post theme - activity sheet. Have it physically in front of you and you will reach so many more new people for your product, service, or business. Our goal is to wake people up on your platform and they need to know that you are here and here to stay. So, posting every day is a must without missing a beat. They need to TRUST that you will be here for a very long time.

So, where does our focus need to be when building a business online? Well, here is what I know... It's very important to not just understand, but to research thoroughly the difference of all the social media platforms I broke down. Once again, these are just a few that I have personally worked with and have been successful on, but that doesn't mean that you couldn't venture out and see if X, formerly known as Twitter, or Pinterest, could work for you. Just remember, it isn't required for you to be on all platforms, but I highly recommend you try to be on most of the platforms because of the diversification and reach.

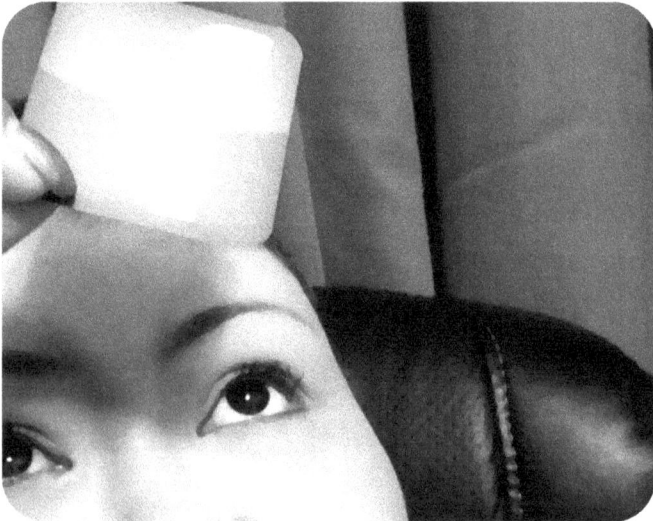

Here are some reasons why some people may not be on Facebook, some may only have Instagram, LinkedIn focuses on business, etc. These platforms all serve a different purpose. This is partly what I love about being diversified. It allows me greater reach and flexibility to find even more people.

Remember, the larger the number of people you get your offer in front of, the better the outcome for business growth. Let's see if I can break it down some more to help you decide what makes the best sense.

When it comes to connecting directly with customers or prospects in specific areas, communities, or interest groups, Facebook and LinkedIn come highly recommended. These are your traditional social networking sites that allow you to amplify your voice through messages and visual content to connect with your audience.

Now, on Instagram, Pinterest, Snapchat, and Tik Tok, they take the lead on visual storytelling, brand building, and social commerce. Having an image-based social media presence is great for offering ways to shop or creating a shopping presence where you can sell directly to your customers through mostly visual content, very heavily picture driven.

When it comes to live streaming on social media, using Facebook LIVE, Instagram LIVE, Tik Tok LIVE and

YouTube are all platforms that broadcast live video to many viewers at once.

Anytime you do a LIVE video stream, Reel, highlight story, Tik Tok video, etc. this format is highly favored and is the going trend for more reach. It is often a bigger reach, and is also viewed more than a regular post, giving you a better chance to find your specific target audience. This should give you more of an in-depth take on the direction in picking the right platform. Some platforms have rules for posting that may not be able to carry over to other platforms. There are some things to keep in mind as you determine the best direction for your strategy with these platforms and how each one has its rules.

Preferably operating as a business under a personal profile is not suggested and ethically not best practice to sell people on. So, first things first, I urge you to create a business page or take your personal profile and turn on the professional mode under your personal account. While professional mode offers similar features, tools and monetization opportunities as a business account, having the professional mode on your personal profile doesn't support management tools or integration with Meta Business Suite currently. Only a business account has that option. When considering marketing yourself online, be sure to invite folks to your business page from your personal page. If you are just going to turn your personal page to professional mode, then you would just work off of that.

Keep all personal matters on your personal profile. This will keep you from confusing your consumers. You can create Facebook ads, boost ads and run them from your business account on your business page or manage in-stream ads on professional mode in the professional dashboard, but unfortunately you will not be able to boost ads and will only have these limited features on professional mode when you become eligible. Of course, none of these features can be done on your personal page.

You can't just blatantly target your friends, new prospects, or target audiences for your business from your personal profile, there is a process. You need to have an attractive professional or business page that is fluid, clean, and helps people understand your brand direction. There is nothing that says you can't build an engagement of friendships on your personal accounts, because essentially isn't that where we should start building relationships first and then invite them to your business page?

That would be the most ethical and respectful way to approach people without crossing compliance on any social media platform. Your Professional and Business page you create allows you the flexibility to link your visitors to a website and contact page that offers your product, service, or opportunity. More importantly, it makes you look more professional.

The best part is that every time you upload a video or create a Facebook live feed or a post, Facebook tracks all of those people who have seen your videos and posts, all of your fans and likes, etc. They collect all of these people into audiences that they call customer audiences, who you can target with ads and marketing periodically.

Keep in mind that it may seem easier just to engage on your personal Facebook profile, not having to transition in moving all your focus and activity onto a professional or business page. Remember, where you put your focus is where you will get the most results.

So, by building relationships on your personal account where most of your friendly personal engagement happens, it frees up the worry of losing a friend to offering something they never asked for.

But building relationships where they will share their needs will open the doors for you, making it that much easier to invite them to check out your business account where you will provide a solution to their need. This is where all business should take place. Remember, nobody wants to be sold to. By engaging genuinely on your personal account and prequalifying them first to see if you should invite them to your business, it will help to create an ethical environment that is organic and not forced into selling. Also keep in mind, your business account provides you with metrics and insight tools to see where you are at with your business that your personal account does not provide. So be sure to know the difference and how each type of profile works in your favor.

So, just like your personal profile, it will take time to build a following; but persistence and consistency is key. When continuing to build friends on your personal Facebook profile always remember to invite them to your business profile every so often. More engagement equals more results.

Sometimes, posting a video or post on your personal page and then enticing them to finish it on your professional or business page (like having a part 2), wanting to learn more about the topic you are discussing, and guiding them on how they can continue receiving more if they want more is a sure way to get their curiosity up and get them following you – if the content is relevant to their needs. It's so important to condition your target audience to meet you on your professional or business page. Teach them to go there more than to your personal profile. By doing this, you can abide by Facebook compliance, and you'll be able to do so much more with your business and your brand direction moving forward.

Ultimately, we are here to build relationships, and sometimes, as mentioned, it's easier to build relationships first on the personal Facebook platform and then invite them, when deemed appropriate, onto the business page. Constantly update your platforms with work, school, favorite books, movies, pictures, etc.

An updated profile shows your friends you are alive, current, and happy with life. People like to work with happy people. Your personal page integrity is just as important, so don't get involved in controversy. People will check out your personal page before they follow your business or professional page, and they will judge your business through your off-duty behavior.

Remember, in your business, you're still selling yourself, not your company. Be careful when adding friends!! Nothing says you can't add friends through mutual relationship growth. But if engaging is done right and you deliver a powerful hook to grab that right prospect, they will chase you down. You won't need to really add friends because they'll be the ones curious and asking you for more information about your offer and can't wait to friend request you.

The people you add have the option to either 'Accept' 'Ignore' or 'Deny' your friend request to add them. If too many people click 'Deny', Facebook will temporarily shut down a few of your features; sometimes, these features could be turned off for weeks at a time, which would be a huge hit to your business for that month.

The features Facebook can block you from using include your messaging and adding more friends. The reason Facebook does this is to prevent "fake" profiles or "spammers" on the site. This is why it's so important to understand why having a business or professional page is better. It is expected to have a higher volume of these kinds of transactions because you are conducting business. You also have a more unlimited following on your business and professional page, unlike your personal profile page, which is limited to the 5000 friends you can have.

A great way to add new friends and communicate with more people is to add yourself to Facebook groups that pertain to your niche. All you do is type in the search bar your niche to look for them. Look over the group first to make sure there is frequent content being added, you don't want to add yourself to a group that hasn't posted in a year. After you are satisfied with the group you have selected, start communicating with people.

Participate in the group often to make yourself familiar to other group members so that later they will want to add you as a friend. Eventually you'll start creating relationships that you'll be able to message them privately with your offer because they asked you for it. You can add yourself to as many groups as you want! The more the merrier; but make sure they are related to your product, service, or opportunity.

Once again, if done right you should never have to chase anyone down or add anyone as friends. THEY will want to add you, creating genuine followers. In today's marketing, we are in a permission-based era and nobody wants to be sold to. If they see that your offer provides a solution they will want to follow you.

START WITH A GOOD HOOK TO GRAB YOUR AUDIENCE'S ATTENTION. Create content with curiosity that would stop people from scrolling on social media. Make sure your content is so catchy, desirable, and memorable that you leave folks wanting to come back for much more.

Have you ever read a book that you couldn't put down and just couldn't wait to read more to get to the good stuff? Well, that's the kind of content you want to create and deliver. Continuously keeping people in suspense will keep them wanting more… keep that in mind.

CREATE RELATABLE CONTENT THAT EVEN STRANGERS YOU DON'T KNOW WOULD CARE HIGHLY ABOUT, STOPPING BY TO VIEW AND READ YOUR MESSAGE. THIS WILL EVENTUALLY LEAD UP TO MAKING FRIENDS AND EARNING LOYAL FANS!

VISUAL QUALITY OF YOUR POST IS KEY

It may not necessarily be as important as the value of the content. As we know, **CONTENT IS KING**, but if the audio or video quality isn't there to complement the content you provide, you could potentially lose your audience's attention and their focus when trying to deliver your message. So be sure the lighting is great, the type of music you use is catchy, information is current and relevant to today's world. Keep unnecessary distractions out of your videos. Don't be boring... yes, be different! Stand out; don't be afraid to be you. Just don't bore your audience. Sharing facts that are entertaining, inspiring, and educational is what most people are looking for today. So always plan before you record to be sure to stay on track with your message and produce a positive outcome. Remember to teach or entertain on a topic that is a common trend that always piques interest and curiosity.

Don't be afraid to learn from other influencers. They are constantly sharing ideas for you to win in your industry. So, check out your competitors and get ideas on how they're doing it.

KEEP YOUR MESSAGE BRIEF AND TO THE POINT.

Everybody has a short attention span, and you don't want to lose their interest. Short, brief content piques curiosity. It gets them remembering you more and interested in wanting to share your valuable content. In fact, if you take a look on social media today, that is all people are doing, sharing content they like. So don't water it down to where you are not worth remembering - or sharing. Refrain from going off on a tangent that doesn't pertain to the subject matter.

If you are posting lengthy messages, make sure there is constant appeal throughout that leaves you wanting more. Keep that constant 'hook' within your message. So be mindful of your content and that it keeps their interest at an all-time high. Being congruent and innovative.

BE SURE TO SHARE YOUR POST TO YOUR STORY AND CREATE REELS.

The bottom line is we want to get your message out there to the masses. Your highlight story and reels are the best way to get more visibility and increase your reach. It's not so much about how many followers you can have, as it is about the connection. The more you post consistent, relevant, exciting, and appealing content, the more you will have loyal fans who can't wait for your next highlight story or reel.

HAVE A CALL TO ACTION... THE SIMPLER IT IS, THE BETTER.

Put out questions and polls to encourage conversation. Give away only the appetizer, not the entire meal!

Leave them wanting more where they will want to sit with you at the table for dinner every time! It's sort of similar to the idea of hooking someone into a TV series, leaving you with a cliffhanger each episode where you can't wait to start the next episode to find out more. Leave your fans with a call-to-action, giving them just enough free information on a subject that will lead them to a "part 2" that they can't wait to sign up for to get the rest of the information because it's so vital to them and their growth.

BE CONSISTENT... BE INTENTIONAL!

I hate to say it, but; in our industry today, people are not consistent with their branding and messaging. It is so important to constantly keep posting video and meaningful marketing content and staying relevant on a daily basis. We want people to find you and know you for your brand, character, content, and consistent effort. You don't have to be fancy about it. Just be clear and concise and make sure it's worth it to them. Would YOU stop scrolling if your message came across your page? Just remember, that consistency is a core fundamental that a leader needs to gain respect, achieve success, establish trust, and inspire confidence in others. So, by applying these important factors to your day-to-day activity, you will find that it will get easier.

Follow the information provided in this chapter to make sure your content is compelling, yet brief; consistent, and relatable, and you will find more people eager to know what you do next. This will ultimately lead to more trust in your message and brand, and more opportunities to connect with more people about your product and opportunity, leading to major increases in your engagements and a successful return. All in all, marketing on any social media platform is about building trust, curiosity and relationships, not spammy ads blasted to everyone with an account.

Remember, the algorithms are changing and the world is evolving right before our eyes. You have to keep up and be aware of the new trends, as we constantly evolve and adapt to the new changes. Social media is getting smarter in the way they want content to be put out. They are now starting to reward those who respect the rules and guidelines and bring authenticity to the masses. They will start opening secret doors allowing you greater reach and visibility. They have moved in this direction more so to eliminate fake accounts, identity stealing, robotic profiles, spammy duplicates, etc. By eliminating these, it allows for a better experience for the end user. So, by constantly posting same content or constantly posting your product, service or opportunity, you are simply selling and social media doesn't like that and they are shifting away from that.

As a matter of fact, they are slowly shutting down accounts that share nothing but other people's content and if your content is shared and used by other people and they don't give you credit for it, these platforms are making sure the original author is given credit for a post someone else made. So, if you think sharing somebody's post or stealing content will get you traction, think again, it's the opposite. Although I have seen in the past how it can really help boost your following by sharing other content as your own, but now, they want originality, organic, authentic content. They have recently started giving true control and credit back to the original author and creator of content, rightfully so. These content creators work very hard on their social media presence to represent who they are, why not? It's giving true content creators a chance to get their posts out to the right people and get their message across. What you're going to start seeing is stricter compliance rules and those who follow suit to it will be the ones that will get more privileges on these platforms. It's as if they've plastered a NO SOLICITING SIGN on people's accounts. So now it's time to be aware and proactive in your marketing efforts.

So, by being intentional about your interest in growing your business online and making sure you are proactive in the set up and on top of your daily responsibilities to the rules of the community, you will find that these platforms can work in your favor. You will notice how quickly these platforms will reward your efforts. This is why we are seeing more people get paid through social media, where your popular "influencers" came from who's had a good head start.

THE PAYOFF IS IN THE EFFORT YOU MAKE TO GET TO KNOW PEOPLE AND TO CULTIVATE A FOLLOWING THAT IS IN LINE WITHIN YOUR NICHE. IT'S ALL ABOUT BUILDNG RELATIONSHIPS AND CONNECTIONS.

CHAPTERSEVEN

GROW YOUR SOCIAL MEDIA PRESENCE

Start by growing a community before you start promoting. The reason to do so is because you have to build trust within your community, and your community needs to trust that you would broadcast useful content that will add value to them. People will only buy from you when they have trusted your business. Only add people you know or people that you've built rapport with! Keep in mind, treat people on these platforms the same way you would want to be treated.

Be careful that you don't create too many friend requests daily on a particular platform.

For example:

Facebook: limits you to a maximum of 20–25 people you can add each day. Any more than that may risk you getting shut down. Adding or requesting no more than 20 people will protect you from the shutdown of features connected to your Facebook page.

LinkedIn: has the same 20-25 connections per day limit, but with a maximum of 100 per week. So, you definitely want to be strategic with that and divide 100 into 7 days if you are going to post every day, 7 days a week.

Instagram: you can follow 200 new accounts within a 24-hour period.

Pinterest: you can follow 20 per day.

Tik Tok: you can safely follow up to 200 users per day, but only 10 new follows per hour.

X (Twitter): you can follow up to 400 per day.

Snapchat: about 20-25 a day.

Profiling is also important when adding friends. Don't just add anybody; look at their profile and see if they might be a good fit for your business or if they could use your product or service. Be careful when networking with busy professionals, whether they are in network marketing or traditional professions. I am not saying that you can't reach out to them, but there is a form of respect in the industry that we all need to adhere to.

Remember, you are unique to YOU. The world has plenty of room and your target audience is waiting specifically for you. So always remind yourself, **THIS IS NOT A COMPETITION!**

Keep in mind that they also have their offer and goal. You don't want to detract them from their business, just like you don't want them to take away from yours. It's still important to support one another, collaborate and lift each other up. Nothing says that you can't be each other's customer. Ultimately, our place is to provide value and a solution for people's needs. You have to be constantly adding value and engagement on your page. Good content would certainly help you to do that. But good content is wasted and ineffective if you don't have a supportive community to broadcast your content to. Content and community need to co-exist; which brings us back to the trust factor. Your audience needs to know you ARE NOT trying to "sell" them. Study your audience so you know when more people are tuned in to you on social media. Be aware if they are not interacting with you, they may be ignoring and avoiding you.

When it comes to social media, past performance and follower activities are equally important. Especially the times your target audience tends to scroll. It's better to pay close attention to the time zones of your target audience and not yours. Look at when your target audience is most active online. This will be the easiest way to figure out the algorithm to maximize your chances of finding the right tribe to deliver your content to and to have a bigger reach and better connection. I would also go as far as to check out your competition and see how they're performing and see what patterns they use that make sense to adjust your frequency, tactics and strategies. When you have a business dashboard, you are able to check your analytics for this. Which is one advantage of having a business account or at least an account under the

BEST TIMES
TO POST

9AM
BREAKFAST

12PM
LUNCH

3PM
AFTERNOON BREAK

6PM
DINNER

9PM
SETTLING DOWN

12AM
LAYING UP IN BED

professional mode status. Sometimes, going back to old, top-performing posts is a great way to determine what other kinds of posts to feature or refurbish. Also consider the awareness of social metrics from high impression, impressive engagement rates, and traffic results. Although you may have success at certain times of the day, it is just as important to optimize and switch up the times occasionally when you are posting just to see what actually provides better engagement. Typically, the "best" times to post in general on all social media platforms, are during prime times. This is when traffic is up. Morning, lunchtime and in the evening at dinnertime and post-midnight hours. When people are at work during the day, they cannot wait to get home and check their social media platforms. So, again this is a generality. You'll be surprised that people are still up scrolling during the midnight hours on social media, so don't exclude that time. I have found that early morning weekdays are the best times. Now, the minute everyone gets out of bed on the weekends, they will reach for their phone, but spend most of their time on it in the mornings. Just give an extra hour since people tend to sleep in on the weekends. Keep in mind, the time can vary per target audience but the best tool to use to monitor and check how your followers are engaging on your post content, stories and reels and increase reach is by checking your professional dashboard under followers and there you will see the graphs that show when your audience is most active.

POST FREQUENCY

PLATFORM	POSTS PER DAY
FACEBOOK	1-2 POSTS 1 HIGHLIGHT STORY 3 REELS
INSTAGRAM	1 POST 2 STORIES/REELS
LINKEDIN	1 POST
PINTEREST	15-25 PINS
TIK TOK	1-4 POSTS
X (TWITTER)	3-4 POSTS
YOUTUBE	1 VIDEO PER WEEK 3 SHORT VIDEOS

POST FREQUENCY is also important to making sure you capture your target audience's attention. The more you post, the more engagement, and the more doors open. But just as posting frequently is important, knowing when and how much is just as important because too much at the wrong times to the wrong people can also hurt your chances of being seen. Here are some recommendations on how often to post on each platform, to see great results:

You can repurpose posts on other platforms, but these platforms prefer you create content using only their interface. It's good practice to create original content for that platform to cater to them and ONLY for them.

Use multiple ways to communicate.

- Try going live; Facebook has created a nifty feature where you can go live on video whenever you please. Even if you don't get a good number of viewers while you are live, Facebook automatically posts the video on your timeline so that people can view it later. So, try going live and personally talk to your audience.

- Comment and message friends DAILY; the easiest way to build rapport with people is to show you care about them. Send personal messages to friends and let them talk to you. Ask them questions. People like to talk about themselves, so always be the listener in the conversation.

- Birthday greetings and celebrations are the best form of communication and a way to send them freebies just to offer a special gift. Don't sell them, but truly provide them with a special gift from your offer that they will appreciate. They will in turn be more inclined to take a look at what you have.

- Frequently like and comment. Engaging on your friends' posts is important. The more you interact with them on their posts, the more they interact with you on yours. This is also good because you'll start to become familiar with their friends whom you communicate with and eventually, they will add you as a friend that you can start conversing your offer with and expand your audience.

- Following up with "likes." When people like your content, be sure to follow-up. Start talking about what you posted or ask what they liked. Be sure that message is sent directly to them and not out in the open where everyone can see your private conversation.

- When messaging friends, try to steer the conversation to address their needs and desires and it will eventually lead them to what you're offering, so see if you can help.

- Be mindful of your friends' time. Don't spam them with group messages about generic business information.

- Don't hype the product, service, or opportunity.

- Speak in words that others can trust. Take your time and share benefits in small amounts, you don't want to overwhelm them.

- Facts tell, but stories sell! Instead of being fact driven about your business, share the emotional side by posting pictures of you at events and telling how they have changed your life. Social proof is what they are looking for.

To sum it up, if it's about an offer, lead them to your business by finding their pain point, their needs and desires. As mentioned earlier, posting frequency is so important. The more you post, the more engagement, and the more doors open. If you are looking to fast track on social media in our fast paced, ever evolving world, then this formula is a sure win! What I've created is a **"21 POST WEEKLY FORMULA RULE"** that works based on frequency metrics and timing that really gets the algorithm stirred up. Post 3 times a day each week, mixing it up - posting 12 unrelated to your offer, posting 7 related benefits (educational) not asking for the sale and 2 call-to-action posts giving them a way to buy. I've noticed that the more you post during prime time with content that is of human interest, the more engagements you will get. This turns into people seeing your content more often. They become more comfortable seeing you in their feed and interacting with you, making it that much easier to lead them to your offer without having to come off as "salesy".

SO... LET'S BREAK DOWN THE FORMULA INTO ITS THREE CATEGORIES TO HELP YOU START GETTING INTERACTIONS.

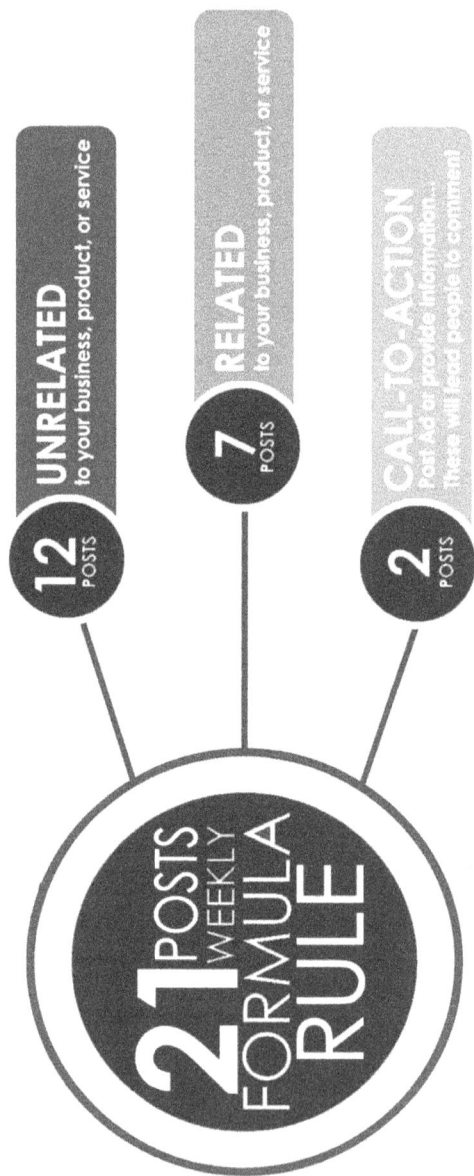

12 POSTS — UNRELATED to your business, product, or service

7 POSTS — RELATED to your business, product, or service

2 POSTS — CALL-TO-ACTION Paid Ad or provide information... (These will lead people to comment)

21 POSTS WEEKLY — FORMULA RULE

12 POSTS) UNRELATED
to your business, product, or service

- "A common belief in our industry that drives me crazy is..."

- "If you had to start a business from scratch today, what would you do or change?"

- "Business is eighty percent about the mind and twenty percent about the grind, do you agree?"

- "Here are my top three favorite business tools right now." (Name your three tools that you can speak on) "Name one of your go-to business tools. Comment below."

- Share a picture of yourself with an inspiring mug or sign.

- Podcast or LIVE video of you and a mentor.

- Ask a question, create a poll, or do a Q&A. (Curiosity driven)

- Repost/share your favorite influencer. (Show you are always learning and becoming better)

- Share a picture of you in your office workplace. (Show you mean business!)

- Post lifestyle and vacation pictures of yourself, friends, family, and loved ones. (Show that you are sociable.)

- Post pictures of yourself speaking at an event but be generic on the post. Like "Love helping people!" or "Love what I do!" (Pique curiosity for people to ask what you do.)

- Picture of an accomplishment on your bucket list.

- Post encouraging quotes and motivational tips.

- Share healthy recipes and ideas.

- Share exercise routines and post pictures of yourself in the gym.

- Do "How to" tutorials.

- Current book you are reading for the month.

- Take a good book and grab training tips from it that will create several more posts about what you learned.

- A special tip of the day or something you learned that was helpful.

- Ask a question and create a debate around it… make it fun, clean, and not too controversial.

- What it's like working as a couple and being around each other a lot.

- What your day looks like working from home.

- Do an interview with one of your top people, favorite influencers, or leaders, etc.

- Do a collaboration with someone about a trending topic?

- Do a video of fun tricks and hacks that pertain to your product or services.

- Post family outing or get togethers.

- Share your wins and successes

7 POSTS **RELATED** to your business, product, or service

- "Something huge is coming! Be sure to stay tuned and watch me here for more updates."

- "I've got something brewing... Hint: Get ready for an exciting announcement in the coming days."

- "You asked for it... I listened! I'm excited to announce the launch of our (___) coming this month. Comment ready below to be the first to get the details."

- "I remember when I was first introduced to (product or service). It helped me with three things. I finally found the time to make this post to share it with you. If you're looking for the same benefits, be sure to drop the word ____if you would like to know more."

- "You + (product) = the perfect match!" Explain

- "My passion is helping people who are struggling with their health (or other issue related to your product/service). If you are ready to get rid of that (problem) comment "ready" and I will DM you."

- (On the way to an event) "Meet me later on my business page to learn more about how lives are changing."

- Name three benefits about your product/service that make sense and then lead them to more information that will blow their mind like a blog link or business page that everyone is talking about.

- "How often do you (target something your product/service benefits) that this can help with?"

- "What's your favorite part of this image?"

- "If you could change one thing about (____) with (benefit of your product/services), what would it be?"

- Drop an emoji in the comments of something relevant to your image, product/services, or brand. Make sure to engage.

- Most of your target audience doesn't know that you can experience (specific) benefit of your product or service. Let them know that you can help.

- "Holy smacks! John got (insert results) from using (product). Learn more about John's journey here." (Link to your blog or a testimonial)

- Tag a friend who needs the benefit of your product and gain an impressive resource who might love the blog.

- "Stop saying you will and start doing it (using product). Are you ready?"

- "I remember when you had the (issue) before using (product/service). It was emotional. I'm so glad that's in the past and now it's changed your life. I share more on the blog here and I hope it adds value to your life, too."

- In one word, describe your product.

- "How many Mondays is it going to take before you decide to get on top of your (issue)?"

- "Want to make (product) easy? Watch three simple tips. Have you tried this before?"

- "Did you know you need to (an action related to your product/service) or there could be negative effects? Make this super easy on yourself and check out my new blog post."

- "Everyone loves free stuff, right? Tag us in your best (workout, food, travel) picture. The contest winner will receive a gift basket of swag." (Provide more contest details.)

- What's your favorite product or service category? Engage with comments and ask if they would like some info on your product/service.

- "Have you ever considered trying a product for (benefit or problem)? If so, are there any contenders?"

- Explain your self-care routine, exercise routine, eating habits, results, etc.

- Name three life choices that led you to your product/service.

- "When I finally started seeing major results of my (product/service), this is how my (business/life) changed. Explain…

- "Even though you've already tried everything under the sun to (benefit). Here's why (product) can work for you.

- The lowest moment of your business and how your product/service helped you come out of it.

- Why time is the only finite resource. It's not money – you can always generate more.

- "Here's why I almost didn't try (product) and why I am glad I did."

- "Want an inside look at being in my world and how my product changed my life?"

- Share before and after pictures of your results.

- "It's so easy to talk about (product) because I know it's helped so many people and also has helped many people make money by simply sharing it."

- The story of why you joined your company.

- "Starting your business can be tricky. It's hard to know where to start and even harder to figure out how to make it grow. No worries, I can help you speed up the process. (Share your secrets on how to grow their business) If you would like more ways to grow your business, comment with "GROW" and I will send you some information about that."

- "As champions, it's always important to be looking for new ways to get the most out of what you're doing. But sometimes, in our quest for growth, we can fall into bad habits that can hold us back. Here are three things you should stop doing right now if you want to achieve (success/results)."

- Just in… "Record breaking month - major life changing stories you don't want to miss!"

- Share the three things and then share a related story about a bad habit you sometimes fall into. "Don't let yourself make the same mistake. I do sometimes, but being aware is an important part of the process."

- "Customer spotlight: (Name)'s journey to (Desired Outcome).

- "Why our product is the perfect gift for any occasion. (Holiday)

- Tips and Tricks on staying motivated

2 POSTS — CALL-TO-ACTION — Post Ad or provide information... These will lead people to comment

- Use marketing ads that lead people to visit a website or you will DM them with information.

- This is where you will throw in that **"buy my product"** featuring your offer for them to fill out a form to sign up that puts them into a drip campaign/funnel system. **This is the only time you would do this!**

Using the ideas I've shared here should help you create some variety in your social media posts without being all over the place. You want to have some consistency in your direction. It's like using GPS to arrive at a targeted destination. You may see many different things along the way, but they all bring you to the same place – your goal! I specifically created this to help bridge the gap from creating content to making your ultimate goal of landing sales and growing your business, preventing the struggle that results in spending too much time and energy putting out content that doesn't get you anywhere.

If you want to be successful in this day and age, you have to be innovative. There is a shift that is happening on social media towards the importance of building your fanbase and creating connections. You have to be constantly adapting, experimenting, and crafting strategies to keep up with the current trends in order for you to be relevant on these platforms today. Testing different theories and ideas is so important to finding that sweet spot that you are looking for that represents who you are or are becoming. When you find it, you will know because it starts to make sense, becomes easier, and adaptation becomes second nature.

If you don't follow the GPS, you may eventually get where you want to go, but more than likely, you'll veer off-course and either waste time and resources, or worse yet, end up in the desert totally lost. People want to see the sights along the way. They want something interesting to interact with. That is why we only post 2 times about buying your product, service or opportunity, out of the 21 posts. The other 19 posts are designed to create curiosity around you and your brand so that when your call-to-action takes place they are more likely to engage because you've dripped enough of a story about you to be intrigued about buying into your offer.

DON'T BE THAT PERSON WHO SHOUTS EVERY DAY ON THEIR SOCIAL MEDIA "COME JOIN OR BUY MY PRODUCT!"

If someone wants to start, they can either scroll through your personal profile and come across your "Call to Action" posts, which won't be difficult to find because it will be a marketing picture or advertisement you created that is catered to having your website information on it or they'll be led to want to look up your bio on your social media platforms and sign themselves up. You've got to love that **NO PRESSURE**

MARKETING! That is the goal! Remember, everybody wants to buy but nobody wants to be sold to. Think about what drew you in to start your business. What got you interested and open to the idea of starting your own business? What did you look for? Take your prospects' feelings into consideration and follow your heart. Better yet, listen to theirs! Don't get so caught up in yourself that you lose sight of your customers' pain points but be of service to your customers and concentrate on solving their problems and fulfilling their needs. Your goal is to catapult your results by making real connections with people that keeps you on their mind, constantly thinking about your offer and the regret they will feel if they don't jump on the opportunity. In turn this will create the ultimate conversion into effortless sales for your business.

Everyone is different when it comes to their approach. You really can't go wrong unless you don't approach them at all. The next chapter, I will go into some simpler conversation starters that can get you moving, warmed up, and get you in front of more people to find the right target audience.

CHAPTER EIGHT

SOCIAL MEDIA POST
CONVERSATION STARTERS

ARE YOU RUNNING OUT OF IDEAS OR HAVING TROUBLE FINDING SOMETHING TO SAY?

Do you tend to post the same thing over and over again, making your profile boring? Or are you posting so many random things that it looks like a hot mess? Building your brand means that you have consistency in your message so that you become known for - and an authority on - your passion. However, to attract people and build interest in your brand you cannot just simply repeat the same pictures, same style, and same quotes.

BE SURE TO MIX IT UP. BE CREATIVE BUT MAKING SURE THAT YOU STAY TRUE TO YOUR MESSAGE.

It can be very challenging to find fresh, new, and current content when posting on social media. But keep in mind that in order to grab someone's attention and to keep them engaged the quality of the content matters. It's like watching a cliffhanger movie. You need to keep people wanting more and wondering what you're going to do next. It has to have continuity in your storyline to keep people on the path. In fact, you can go so far to say that we are story tellers of our lives without getting into too many real-life details.

"LIKE" THEIR POST

TAG A FRIEND

SHARE THEIR POST

COMMENT SOMETHING NICE (5 WORDS OR MORE)

SOCIAL MEDIA MARKETING

LEAVE A REVIEW

COMMENT AN EMOJI

POST A PIC (FUN ACTIVITIY & SPECIAL EVENT)

SHOUT THEM OUT!

Here are some content and branding examples to help expand your message and keep you focused:

- Videos - one of the highest traffic generators - these are previously recorded and uploaded, like YouTube, Stories, IGTV, TikTok, Reels.

- Live videos - doing in real time, notifies your audience immediately and generates urgency.

- Showcase your customers and business partners - builds trust in what you do.

- Articles and blog posts - entice people to cross media and connect with you on your website/social media.

- Share Influencer content you follow from an authority that fits with your brand.

- Your biggest win or biggest mistake in your industry - shows that you have experience.

- Carousels, gifs, and animations - take advantage of people looking at your content for a longer period of time.

- Product and service photos - showcase your product WITHOUT selling, especially a 'sneak-peak' or upcoming product launch.

- Polls and surveys - promote two-way engagement. Everybody loves being asked their opinion.

- Press releases or mentions in the media - is like a third-party verification that also builds trust.

- Things people don't know about you - generates curiosity so that people want to get to know you.

- Repost your best post from last year - view your insight tools to find a post that had a great response. If it generated results before, it will do it again and attract more people.

- Screenshot a quote written on a sticky note, whiteboard, or text conversation - shows that everything isn't rehearsed, planned, or generated by someone else. Some of your best messages are things that inspire you.

I know trying to come up with ideas on what to post on a daily basis can be tough, especially if it's your first time on social media. The thing to keep in mind is that you have to truly be intentional with your posts and not derail yourself on the concept of posting that you lose sight of the topic at hand and lose the engagement with your potential prospects.

Better yet you're so caught up in the work that you're not engaged in conversations, that you're not making any sense or connecting the call-to-action goal. We get so heads down, blinders on posting away, and no call-to-action or buyers for that matter. It is so important to understand that no matter the idea and topic, the sole direction is to find a way to converse and these post ideas will have a way to convert them in the end.

If you share a step-by-step tutorial, are you able to use that topic to lead them to introducing your product, service, or opportunity? Your goal should be to try to convert them by asking relevant questions from that topic, leading them to your offer.

So be intentional with your post ideas so that you are able to convert them to a call-to-action. Otherwise, you will not be able to maximize these platforms to engage and generate leads that can turn into potential buyers.

The key to effectively get prospects is to listen and engage in the responses and interact intentionally. Interacting is vital, it's our follow-up that is key! I would rather see you post quality engaging content less frequently than to put up meaningless posts just to get your posts in for the day to hit your frequency goals. Now, if all the content I've provided so far in this book regarding fast tracking on social media seems overwhelming, and you're having a hard time hitting the ground running, here's my simplified <u>once</u> a day *"30 DAYS OF SOCIAL MEDIA POST IDEAS"*.

Posting something of value once a day is better than giving up and not posting at all. This cheat sheet is to help take the guesswork out so that you can start interacting and getting things moving until you are comfortable to post more frequently and dive into the **21 POST WEEKLY FORMULA.** These post ideas are just suggestions that you can refer to. It may also help to stir up some ideas for new content to come up with that you may not have thought of before and even more ideas that may not even be listed here. Use it to ensure that you are spreading out your topics, but not straying off course.

Keep in mind, this is just a general list to give you some ideas. You will still need to cater them to your niche in some way. I would go so far as to customize this template and create one for your business specifically. There are more topics that you can add to this as you get the hang of it. You will be surprised as to how much you can come up with and how creative you really are. But for now, this will give you a good 30 day run to get in the habit of posting your content daily. I have kept the content as generic as possible to cater to the general masses.

The goal is to try to come up with content that is catchy, gains curiosity and interest. There are some apps you can download that can help create videos and reels, as well as, using A.I. to assist but not to take over your content creation but to help you perfect your message. Remember, you want to be authentic in your posts, be careful when using apps or A.I. that it doesn't come off robotic or not sounding like you at all. Be different, be creative, and add value so that you stand out!

Always plan your content ahead of time to stay on schedule with posting. These post ideas don't have to be in the order shown. Just make sure you are current.

30 DAY SOCIAL MEDIA POST IDEAS

1 PICTURE WITH INSPIRING MUG/SIGN	2 MORNING HEALTH REGIMEN DRINK	3 FAVORITE BUSINESS RESOURCE/ TOOL	4 CREATE A POLL OR Q&A.	5 MORNING BUSINESS ROUTINE
6 PROMOTE EXCLUSIVE OFFER	7 BUSINESS SHOUT OUTS	8 SHARE FAVORITE PRODUCT	9 SHARE A PRODUCT TESTIMONY	10 PICTURE OF YOU IN YOUR OFFICE
11 INSPIRING QUOTE	12 TRAINING ARTICLES YOU TEACH	13 LIFESTYLE VACATION PICTURES	14 PICTURE OF YOU PUBLIC SPEAKING	15 PICTURE OF YOU AT A BIG EVENT
16 WEEKEND PLANS/ GETAWAY	17 SECRETS, CASE STUDIES AND TIPS	18 PRODUCT BENEFITS AND TIPS	19 PROMOTE OFFER OR FREEBIE	20 SELFIE WORDS ON PICTURE
21 WISH LIST/ BUCKET LIST	22 MORNING EXERCISE ROUTINE	23 HOLIDAY SPECIALS	24 INTERVIEW LEADER OR TEAMMATE	25 WORKING POWER COUPLE
26 TUTORIALS "HOW TO"	27 STORY BLOGS OR REPURPOSE CONTENT	28 SPECIAL TIP OF THE DAY OR EVENING	29 GROUP/ TEAM PICTURES	30 CURRENT BOOK YOU ARE READING

The goal on social media is to attract that perfect buyer and grab their attention, hook that lead, and convert them into a fan. Now, it's not enough to just ask a question or post something like, "What does your bucket list look like?" because now, how will you convert them to your product offer or opportunity offer from this question. I know that although when you hook a lead, they may be at the very top of your mind in your sales funnel; but don't be fooled by their interest level.

While they are aware of your company and your product, they have not been qualified yet, and it won't be clear how promising they are as a potential lead looking to buy. Alternatively, prospects are leads who have been QUALIFIED and deemed likely to buy. We want to be sure to grab that person's attention, hook that lead, and convert them into a follower and a fan that becomes a prospect that ends up as a sale for you. Know the difference between a lead and a prospect. To do that, you must create your brand story by connecting with people on a personal level. Once again, it's all about building that personal relationship and engaging with them using your brand stories to promote your product, service, or opportunity in your marketing efforts to appeal to your tribe and raving fans. One thing I have learned is that everyone today is cautious about their time and money. "What's in it for me, and why should I join you?" If you cannot make someone feel good about that, forget about it – Game Over! Let's face it… If you are not providing something of value that tugs at their main pain points, how can you expect them to support your concept, business or ideas? Better yet, how can they believe you are about them, when you keep displaying that it's about you and the sale? Many times, we get caught up in the sale instead of what we can do to help them, just to find out later they are already thinking about refunding or cancelling the order.

So, I put together a **BONUS** just for you, YES, I am divulging one of my favorite blueprints that converts, I put it together in a way that is easy to understand and help to convert your clients every time. That is *"The COOKIE TRAIL FORMULA."* It's my simple outline, leading them to a call-to-action helping you avoid future failures by creating a solution to clients' or customers' problems. The goal is to get them to eat the cookie (close the sale) and not have trails of cookie crumbs (doubters and non-buyers).

THE COOKIE TRAIL FORMULA
The Ultimate Blueprint that converts

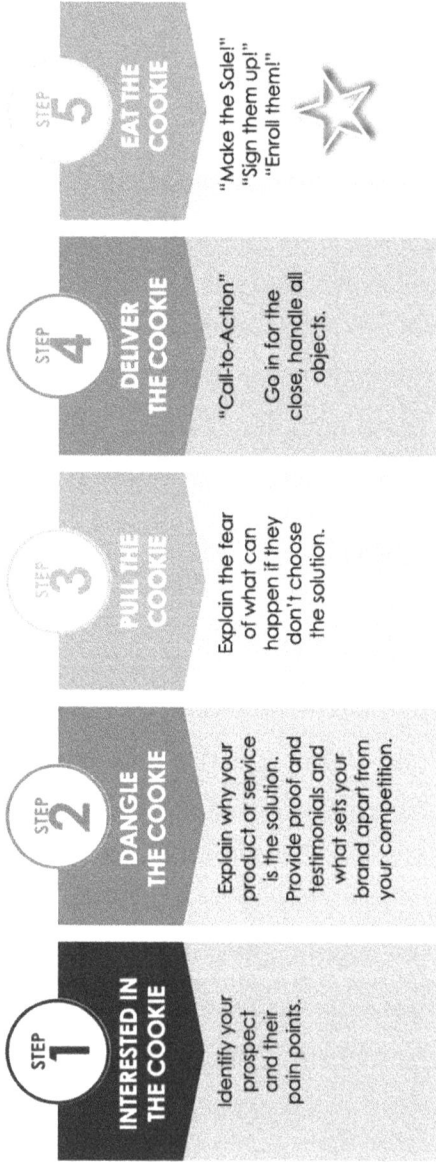

STEP 1
INTERESTED IN THE COOKIE

Identify your prospect and their pain points.

STEP 2
DANGLE THE COOKIE

Explain why your product or service is the solution. Provide proof and testimonials and what sets your brand apart from your competition.

STEP 3
PULL THE COOKIE

Explain the fear of what can happen if they don't choose the solution.

STEP 4
DELIVER THE COOKIE

"Call-to-Action"

Go in for the close, handle all objects.

STEP 5
EAT THE COOKIE

"Make the Sale!"
"Sign them up!"
"Enroll them!"

CHAPTER NINE

SOCIAL MEDIA
DO'S AND DON'TS

- Don't have 2 or more brand identities going on at once. Pick your brand and go with that. Know it. Fans should be able to take pride in following your page. You never want to confuse them when you are introducing multiple offers. If you are a company with several offers, create separate accounts for them so you can cater to the right target audience.

- Be careful not to over-post on nonrelevant or uninteresting content that does not have continuity!! Spamming someone's social media wall is a sure way to get them uninterested in ANYTHING you decide to post.

- Do not neglect your BIO and PROFILE

- Don't buy your "Likes" and "Followers".

- Post lifestyle pictures often; people are more inclined to look at pictures than read a paragraph.

- Stay positive; people generally add happy people into their friendship circle and like to keep the negativity away.

- Post motivation; people like to be uplifted, and a simple motivational post could draw a bigger audience your way. Everyone likes feeling good!

- Post only relevant topics that people want to share. Post using relevant news, trending topics, and current events.

- Stay away from controversial topics; politics, religion, etc. are things people are very passionate about. You don't want to start a debate with anyone because there's a difference of opinion. Keep it neutral.

- Do not post offensive content. This will be a good way to get shut down. Remember, building relationships requires trust and we don't want to compromise our integrity or character.

- Do not post your corporate website; this is an automatic red flag to your audience that you are trying to sell them.

- Website links should be saved for individual, private conversations or in your bio.

- Post mostly images and upload videos directly to the specific platform that caters to your audience. Your job is to keep your audience staying on your particular platforms. It doesn't like you leading them to another platform.

- Posting marketing pertaining to your product; when posting content about your company's product, make sure you are compliant. Do not make any miracle claims, and you can't use someone else's testimony without their permission.

- Share your excitement about your business. Your posts should be 80% adding value to their needs and 20% business related per week. Share your excitement about your business! Talk from the heart when posting.

- Don't focus on "make money with me" posts; focus most of your time on further developing relationships with your Facebook network. Most will be curious about the results.

- Be consistent. Not posting daily is not good, so if it's about making the time, be sure to create content ahead of time and use the content calendar, and schedule posts in advance.

- Stay up to date and relevant on current trends.

These are just few of the "Do's and Don'ts" of social media. Keep in mind, as you move along in your business, you will find what works and what doesn't to be effective on social media for your brand direction. Just make sure you are compliant!

Here's an example of a Social Media Checklist to help remind you of some of your daily activities on your various social platforms to help maximize marketing efforts. Be sure to cater it to your niche and add to what is here.

SOCIAL MEDIA
CHECKLIST

✓ Respond to ALL incoming messages

✓ Check your comments, mentions, notifications and DMs.

✓ Monitor your social media for keywords and phrases

✓ Schedule posts ahead of time to free up your time

✓ Scroll through platforms for inspiration

✓ Post meaningful content that will stop them from scrolling

✓ Engage with posts that are relevant to yours

✓ Always be brainstorming and working on new ideas

✓ Attend chats, hangouts and groups

CHAPTER TEN

ATTRACTION MARKETNG
THAT GENERATES LEADS

We are now seeing a trend that young adults who have gone to college are still having to find a side hustle to pay off student debts. By the time they are able to do that, they are finding that they have gotten good at their side gig and make as much or more than what they have gone to school for. Just to realize that what they went to school for isn't what they love to do, it's actually what they are currently doing instead.

The same could be said for an individual who is supposed to be retired but can't and has to find a business to supplement income.

The idea is to create retirement income that has true retention. But the scary thought is that we know we have to have a business with a huge demand but has to have merits for sustainability. Otherwise, that too could be what's also holding you back in the growth process. How do we provide curiosity for a product if we don't market it with a demand? To maintain raving fans, they need to know THEY NEED OUR OFFER, PRODUCT OR SERVICE. We are in a fast-paced world of people who want it now, a quick fix, quick way, easy money. But will that last? The question really remains, what will it take to be the best?

The competition can be grueling. For example, top leading in the industry is "beauty" and "health and wellness." How do you compete with that? There are so many. I can remember someone saying, "I can't possibly compete as a newbie." I am here to tell you that what is going to set you apart from your competition is YOU and your authenticity. There are plenty of people to go around, and your tribe is out there. Just be yourself and not like everyone else. Don't be such a copycat out in the industry. I believe in regurgitating great information but **do it your way**...stand out from the crowd.

HERE'S FOOD FOR THOUGHT...

When you go to the grocery store, and you go down the bread aisle, how do you possibly choose from all the different types of bread? Better yet, how do they stay in business with the competition? The reality is there is a buyer for all of them. It's in how they have positioned themselves in the marketplace and how their marketing campaigns cater to a particular individual. Now, although that is great that we market to a particular target audience, we also have to be transparent in the way that we market, in fear that we limit ourselves and lose the masses. One thing we want to keep in mind is that we want to be able to have a captive audience. We want to attract a number of people based on many things such as demographics, location, gender, age, etc. Be diverse. Remember, you may have an offer, product, or service that everyone needs, but will only cater to certain people based on how you market and how you present yourself that will be attractive to your particular audience.

For example, how we dress can be an indicator of what crowd we attract, your lingo, how you carry yourself, and how you speak. If you are quiet and timid, or loud and spunky, you will attract certain target audiences. So, if we are to just cater to the few because we can't be transparent, we could lose a good number of people.

In general, it may be good practice to make a few adjustments to cater to as many people as possible. But if they are seeing you as an educator of your product and/or service never portraying your side of anything and always putting them first in their needs, you will get their attention every time.

Nobody wants to be sold to. They just want to be heard with their challenges and concerns. If you can provide them with a solution to their problem, focusing on only that... you will win your prospect over every time... SCORE!!

SO, WHAT DOES YOUR MARKETING CAMPAIGN LOOK LIKE? There are so many ways you can market your business online or offline. There is so much valuable information on methods that work so why try to reinvent the wheel?

Again, I cannot emphasize it enough. Just follow those who have gone before you; emulate and implement. Learn to be the master of regurgitating great information.

Take what you learn and recreate it in your teaching style and theme in mind. I can promise the leaders that you hear today learned from the leader before them. Of course, always give credit where it is due when it comes to quotes and sayings.

More and more people look for simplicity, to work smart, not hard, and to be effective because of the way the world has shifted from such a hustle and bustle mentality that most everybody wants everything to be easy and accessible, a no-nonsense approach that they wouldn't have to think about it, figure it out or have to worry about it. Everything has gone from hotels to Airbnb, taxis to Ubers and Lyft's. So be sure to cater your marketing to that of your target audience, marketing that appeals to the masses based on your product and the service you offer.

I have been in this industry for over 25 years, and what used to be the way I would do my marketing campaigns from a local traditional marketing sense before I even hit the social media marketing scene - believe it or not, I still use some of those local marketing campaigns today - even taking that to the internet. It really just depends on your company. They definitely have their place in certain situations and can truly be helpful.

THE DIFFERENCE BETWEEN ONLINE AND OFFLINE MARKETING IS THAT OFFLINE TRADITIONAL MARKETING TALKS AT PEOPLE CONTENT MARKETING TALKS WITH THEM.

I highly recommend, in addition to social media marketing, which is huge in itself, which I just shared, that you also want to have at least ten local traditional marketing campaigns going at one time. Even though social media marketing is indeed the fastest way to grow. I have learned that the local traditional marketing, belly to belly relationships, has produced me several rockstars that I have never met before, who have become part of my family tree. So don't dismiss that way of marketing so quickly. Everyone is so fixated on the internet, and rightfully so. Who doesn't want to have it now, quickly and make more money fast, right? The change towards digital and content marketing strategies has become a huge shift and is gaining momentum in the marketplace today.

So, I can totally understand that the era of local traditional marketing is dying. But also keep in mind as everyone is trying to figure out this online marketing world, all the while, the local traditional marketing that still works if you use the right marketing campaign, is completely wide open.

Being diverse and learning to tap into several marketing campaigns can mean the difference in the outcome of various prospecting outlets and provide a greater reach to more markets to move into, creating more avenues and options to finding that ideal customer, client or prospect to introduce your product, service or opportunity.

Here are some **local traditional marketing campaign** ideas that still work today:

- Word of mouth (3ft rule)
- Business cards, sizzle cards, flyers and postcards
- Vehicle magnet/vinyl signs
- In-person B2B
- Email and phone leads
- Educational seminars
- At home events
- Church fundraisers
- School fundraisers
- Social events
- Vendor events
- Chamber of Commerce
- BBB membership
- Collaboration and referrals
- Podcasts and interviews
- Hotel speaking events
- Newsletter ads with apartment complex
- Assisted living residences newsletters
- Assisted living residence seminars
- Homeowners' welcome wagon

Once again, these are just to name a few, but you get the idea. I think we tend to dismiss these local traditional marketing campaigns because, let's face it, as mentioned, social media is the fastest and surest way to reach out to a huge mass number of people.

We can definitely incorporate these things because they still work; it can't hurt but adds to your business.

BE CONSISTENT AND READY TO ADAPT AS NEEDS CHANGE!

You need to have several of these at your disposal and working for you. Many times, what's hot in your marketing changes.

That doesn't mean that you should focus on just that one method. You never know when one way is going to yield results, and another grows cold. You want to always be moving forward, and anything that yields even one prospect to get you closer to your goal is valuable. Don't complicate it. When we make it harder on ourselves than what it really is, we start to feel stumped.

Just remember we are constantly selling ourselves and we don't even know it. Have fun in the process! The key here is to be consistent in your marketing efforts. Whether you're going to send out a weekly newsletter with tips or special offers, maybe you'll have a social media ad (two or three) with a daily number of people you want to reach.

Perhaps you'll have a highlight or special offer on your website that you need to broadcast across several channels and platforms (think YouTube, Facebook, Instagram, TikTok, Email).

Just remember to meet people where they are at. People have different likes and different preferences. Some people spend their life on electronics and online, while other people may not be so tech savvy or simply refuse to be on any social media platforms

So, by investing your efforts in different avenues, even the ones you may not be personally drawn to, you'll reach the maximum number of people who can benefit from what you offer.

WHATEVER IT IS THAT YOU DECIDE TO DO WITH MARKETING YOUR BUSINESS, DON'T RELY ON JUST ONE METHOD. BE SURE TO DIVERSIFY!

What I have learned in the 25 years of being in business for myself is that being diversified in my marketing efforts helped me to see what worked and what didn't work for my particular brand, allowing me to focus on what really is effective with advertising to my niche, gauging my specific metrics online and offline to concentrate on what works best.

When it comes to marketing there is no one size fits all. The cookie cutter mentality just doesn't work. For example, the system I mentioned earlier, "The Cookie Trail Formula", does work but you are the secret ingredient. If you don't put yourself into your marketing then your cookie will be bland and lifeless. Nobody wants to buy a tasteless cookie.

As a matter of fact, if you ask anyone about buying a cookie from the grocery store, they all kind of taste the same. But take a homemade cookie for instance, that will be the most preferred choice. Don't get me wrong, though the store-bought cookies are consistent, they are something everyone can expect with no originality. Now, a homemade cookie is unique and will create a buzz for people to want to go out of their way for and purchase. People come to me all the time saying they need a side gig, and once they try it, they come back saying that it didn't work. **It's not that the company, product, services or opportunity didn't work...**YOU DIDN'T WORK... You didn't make it your own.

Remember, what you do on a daily basis becomes your maximum potential. So as long as you are creating the campaigns that produce the income, planting the seed daily, then, you can feel good knowing that harvest is coming. You will reap what you sow. So, get in the habit of having daily disciplines in place, be ahead of it and your business will continue to soar. Stay current, be innovative and keep your funnel full so that your business will never grow stale.

Bottom line... the factors that go into your marketing efforts all have to align to who you are as a brand, how people see you through your engagements and commitments, marketing campaigns and delivering the message in a way that connects, c**reating a community that will become YOUR TRIBE!**

Your time to pop is approaching, now it's up to you to take what you've learned here and run with it!

CONCLUSION

CONGRATULATIONS!
YOU ARE NOW IN BUSINESS

You are finally in business my friend…

Ready to market and take on the world. Now, whether you are a busy professional, network marketer, or business owner, most of how you market yourself is similar.

IMPLEMENT WHAT YOU HAVE LEARNED HERE AND CREATE FINANCIAL SECURITY THAT YOU CAN CALL YOUR OWN!

When you follow these critical steps and focus on your identity and what you want to be known for, and you stay true to your passion, it will be that much easier to stay on course with your business goals. Build a business that has a high retention that will last and be of service to your customers to create long lasting friendships and raving fans.

Remember, love everyone where they are at and meet them at their needs. We want to provide our customers with every possible solution to their problem a light of hope. Give 100% with zero expectations and stop chasing the money. The money will come when you serve where you are needed and bless others first! So, as you grow in your business, be sure to grab testimonies and proof of your work along the way.

This is huge when you are talking to clients, whether they get this from social media, a website, an advertisement, etc. Positive recognition helps people who don't know you yet trust that you can deliver on your product or service.

Word of mouth is still one of the most important ways to grow your business and gain clients. Negative word-of-mouth advertising can also kill your business no matter how much advertising you do.

The more positive experiences and testimonies you can gather and showcase, the more organic business you can receive and the more opportunities you have to create long-lasting, repeat customers.

Most of what I am sharing here with you is what was shared with me throughout my 25+ years of being a successful business owner. I owe a lot of my success to the legacy leaders that I have met or partnered with along the way. I have always plugged myself into daily **PERSONAL DEVELOPMENT, IT IS A MUST** to keep up with the ever growing and changing industry. Personal development is not only mental, but emotional and physical as well.

Don't ever go it alone. If you think that you know everything and that you have arrived once you hit the top, or your company is starting to take off, you're mistaken! To be successful, you will need to 'plug in' to something bigger than yourself always and lead your team to something bigger than YOU. Don't allow ego to manifest in your success. Always be willing to learn, seek advice from the best who walked before you, and become a student. When you are at the top of the chain, and you're the only lifeline, plugging into personal development can keep you motivated and educated - each aspect feeds the other.

The industry is forever changing, and there is always something to learn about your industry. To be the authority and master in what you do requires constant personal growth and education. Now, there is an endless supply of well-known authors in personal development, motivation, marketing, and more. Plus, new up and coming rising influencers who have really taken the industry by storm with the current marketing trends online. They too will tell you, it's a must to always feed the mind and educate yourself daily. You have to make sure you're always keeping up with your competitors.

When I first started in network marketing, I would hear people say, "why do only 10% of people make it to the top of their industry?" Ever wonder why? Truth is, because they underestimate the work that will be required, and they go into it with the wrong attitude.

We have to be emotionally intelligent and invested. It's imperative when building your success in the industry. You have to be able to have the ability to identify and manage your own emotions as well as the emotions of others. It really requires you to understand yourself and others better. Because everything you do relies on building and engaging relationships.

Practice using and incorporating one thing from what you read into your day. Consciously integrating things that you learn immediately helps reinforce those patterns in your mind and body so that they become your norm and become second nature.

3.. 2.. 1.. THE CUTTING OF THE RIBBON HAS NOW COMMENCED AND YOU JUST OPENED OR REOPENED YOUR DOORS, OR YOUR ONLINE BUSINESS HAS LAUNCHED AND BUSINESS WILL NOW BE BOOMING!

I am so excited for your launch. Surely now, you can see that what you offer is in fact what everyone needs but most importantly, YOU are in control, in a league of your own, and no one can compete with your unique authenticity to become the best in your industry. Envision it… see yourself already there, my friend. **The best is yet to come!**

FINAL WORD

KNOWING IS NOT ENOUGH

CONGRATULATIONS ROCKSTAR!!

Now that you have finished reading my book, it's time to implement what you've learned! Be sure to keep this step-by-step guide and foundational principles handy so that you can refer back to it. I warned you that this book will make you crush it in your industry, providing you with the arsenal and the power to be successful. But keep this in mind, although knowledge is key, it has no power. You won't give it any if you don't implement it. You can finally feel good that you can make sense of it all and not get sick of the daily grind, instead finally love what you do, win at every level and get ahead in life! Start getting excited! I am so glad that I can serve in a capacity where we can all win together!

IF YOU ARE STILL FEELING STUCK, WHY WAIT UNTIL YOUR BACK IS UP AGAINST THE WALL? DO SOMETHING ABOUT IT?

If you would like that one-on-one attention, personal coaching and mentoring by me to help completely put this into perspective and implement all this into action right away... Be sure to visit my website: and "get on the list" for early access to the latest training, resources and tools, promotions and more.

Let's take you from a busy rock-bottom professional to a **ROCKSTAR** entrepreneur today and **BUILD A BRAND NEW YOU!**

CONNECT WITH JENNIFER
www.JenniferWelch.com

ADDITIONAL RESOURCES

BUILD A BRAND NEW YOU! - EBOOK DOWNLOAD AND FLIPBOOK ACCESS

BRANDING AND SOCIAL MEDIA PACKAGE AND ONE-ON-ONE CONSULTING

DONE 4U BRAND WEBSITE WORDPRESS AND SEO OPTIMIZED

BUILD A
BRAND
NEW YOU!

STEP BY STEP GUIDE TO
LAUNCHING A SUCCESSFUL BUSINESS

JENNIFER JW WELCH

www.ingramcontent.com/pod-product-compliance
Lightning Source LLC
Chambersburg PA
CBHW040921210326
41597CB00030B/5145